KU-605-458

South Dublin Libraries

www.southdublinlibraries.ie

NAKED

Caroline Foran is a number one bestselling author, freelance lifestyle journalist and creator of the chart-topping podcast *Owning It*.

Caroline lives in Dublin and prior to her career in media, she obtained a degree in Communications and a master's in Film & Television Studies, both from Dublin City University.

Also by Caroline Foran
Owning It: Your Bullsh*t-Free Guide to Living with Anxiety
The Confidence Kit: Your Bullsh*t-Free Guide to Owning Your Fear

Naked:
Ten Truths To Change Your Life

CAROLINE FORAN

HACHETTE
BOOKS
IRELAND

Copyright © 2021 Caroline Foran

The right of Caroline Foran to be identified as the Author of
the Work has been asserted by her in accordance with the
Copyright, Designs and Patents Act 1988.

First published in Ireland in 2021 by
HACHETTE BOOKS IRELAND

2

All rights reserved. No part of this publication may be reproduced, stored in
a retrieval system, or transmitted, in any form or by any means without the
prior written permission of the publisher, nor be otherwise circulated in any
form of binding or cover other than that in which it is published and without
a similar condition being imposed on the subsequent purchaser.

Cataloguing in Publication Data is available from the British Library

ISBN 9781529352146

Typeset in Neutraface Slab Text by www.grahamthew.com

Printed and bound in Great Britain by
Clays, Elcograf S.p.A

Hachette Books Ireland policy is to use papers that are natural, renewable and
recyclable products and made from wood grown in sustainable forests. The logging and
manufacturing processes are expected to conform to the environmental regulations of the
country of origin.

Hachette Books Ireland
8 Castlecourt Centre
Castleknock
Dublin 15, Ireland

A division of Hachette UK Ltd
Carmelite House, 50 Victoria Embankment, EC4Y 0DZ

www.hachettebooksireland.ie

Contents

Introduction 1

Truth #1 You'll never have it all figured out 11

Truth #2 There's nothing easy about
changing your life 23

Truth #3 You can do anything, but you
can't do everything....................................... 55

Truth #4 Where there is failure, there is
always opportunity 87

Truth #5 A willingness to be vulnerable
makes you invulnerable: understanding
the vulnerability paradox 103

Truth #6 Not everyone will like you 127

Truth #7 Someone else's success
does not take from yours 159

Truth #8 If you want to be happy,
you're doing it wrong 185

Truth #9 Trust your instincts –
you have them for a reason 213

Truth #10 There is no end goal 229

Conclusion 245

Acknowledgements 249

Notes 251

For Caelan, my beautiful baby boy who came along just before going to print with this book.

Introduction

HELLO DEAR READER and welcome to my third book, *Naked: Ten Truths To Change Your Life*.

What's it all about?

And is nudity really a prerequisite for getting on board?

Let's get the latter out of the way first. No. It is only in an emotional sense that this book will require you to disrobe – you just won't get anything out of it if you hide behind any sort of pretence – but, by all means, feel free to strip down to your birthday suit if that's what makes you feel good. (I only ask that you don't flood my DMs with selfies, please.)

To answer the first question, allow me to give you a little bit of background.

In picking up this book, I assume that, like me, you are interested in understanding more about why we are the way we are. Why we think and feel and behave in the ways that we do, and what we can do to increase the volume on the good stuff in our lives while, at the same time, turning down the dial on, well, there's no better way to put it: the shit stuff. I think it's fair to say that, in general, when it comes to personal development, and the very driving force behind why we gravitate towards these kinds of self-help books, we're concerned with getting our lives together in such a way that enables us to live a good one. That's what it's always been about for me, anyway: making life easier and more enjoyable.

To bring you up to speed on where I'm at and what inspired this book, let's start with a little visualisation exercise.

I want you to imagine this idea of getting your life together, which we'd all like to do if we're not already doing it, in the same way as you'd approach the seemingly insurmountable task of cleaning out your house - room by room. Throughout my twenties and into my early thirties, I've been engaged pretty much full-time in this clear-out project. There have been some speed bumps along the way - think of those piles of tangled Christmas lights which you look at and think, *I'll probably die before I ever manage to sort these out* - but I'm proud to say that I've had some success in clearing through what I would describe as the more significant piles of crap that held me back for so long.

For one, I can say that I've got to a point of owning my anxiety so that it doesn't own me (as chronicled in my first book, *Owning It*). That was a big one.

For another, I've karate-chopped through my fear of failure, allowing for courage and lasting self-confidence (all of which you'll find chronicled in book two, *The Confidence Kit*). Another biggie.

I've also learned to work with what I've got, rather than what I don't have. This is, in and of itself, a game-changer and means I can create the best possible experience for myself.

Having got these tasks out of the way (and don't let me sugarcoat it; it took a long bloody time and also requires regular maintenance), I then found myself left with the task of clearing out those last few drawers of annoying why-am-I-still-holding-on-to-this clutter. Those bits of crap that are always there, that we tend to overlook, that we know we should face but find umpteen reasons not to. We think, *I'll get to that some day*, and, of course, we never do.

For me, these are the seemingly innocuous blockages that stand between us and total clarity. It's the one cupboard you've yet to address and while there may be no sense of urgency to do so – what's in there isn't necessarily preventing you from living your life – you just know you'll feel a lot more calm and more at ease when you do.

You'll create more space where you live, and where you live is in your mind and body.

In my version of this cupboard, you'll find things such as old batteries, more lint rollers than it's ever necessary to own – no wait, that's the actual contents of my random-shit drawer. In my proverbial drawer, you'll find the likes of imposter syndrome, people-pleasing behaviours, jealousy and envy, social comparison, a tendency towards burnout – any and all of these super fun things.

What's in your cupboard may differ from what's in mine but from what I've learned, it seems these kinds of items are pretty common. And they bother us. They create stress in our lives, adding to a constant hum of anxiety that starts to become our new normal. They build up over time and, even though we try our best to deny them and look the other way – for example, automatically thinking someone else's bad mood is your fault – eventually, we can't ignore the negative impact these things, these behaviours, are having on us.

Unfortunately, though, addressing what's in this imaginary cupboard, along with everything else you might already have faced in your life thus far, isn't always a comfortable process. It's hard work and it requires a lot of energy. What's more, these aren't habits or behaviours we've learned overnight, so we can't expect to unlearn them overnight either.

It requires us to really look inside ourselves to see what's not working for us and then have the courage to change it or the guts to get rid of it.

In my own attempts at clearing through these things, I've realised that what's really required to get the job done is this: a willingness to be vulnerable.

We need to allow ourselves to be vulnerable in order to look at what we've got and what we're dealing with. We need to become vulnerable if we're to really ask ourselves why we are the way we are and why we do the things we do, before we can make a change.

Why, you ask, does this require vulnerability?

Because we might not like what we find. We won't want to admit, for example, that we struggle to celebrate others' success because it threatens our own. Nobody wants that plastered on their Twitter bio but staring down the barrel of this truth and confronting it in order to change it is what must be done, and in order to do that we need to allow ourselves permission to be vulnerable.

Interestingly, the more I thought about vulnerability as being the essential ingredient for achieving any kind of personal development, the more it emerged to me as the most obvious and unavoidable theme that would bring this whole book together.

I'll go into far more detail on the power and definition of vulnerability in Chapter 5. For now I only ask that you open yourself up to the idea of vulnerability - which, to me, involves being the most authentic version of yourself rather than the curation of your best bits that go on social media. The you that's how you are, as you are, when you are and not how you think you should appear. Get this part right, even if it's just between you and me for now, and you'll soon reap the rewards.

To get the most out of this book, you will need to join me in peeling back your own layers. I won't lie, at first, it's uncomfortable as fuck (hence my freak-out at the beginning of the Chapter 1), but I promise you this: soon it will become as liberating as frolicking along a nudist beach, assured in the knowledge that everyone else is too busy looking at their own jiggly bits to be remotely concerned with yours.

By the book's close, my hope is that you'll no longer perceive vulnerability as something to fear but as something that brings you closer to your truest self, something that just might hold the key to your well-being and, dare I say it, your happiness too.

So, vulnerability. This is what I mean by the nakedness in the book's title – it is our central theme.

But what of the book's structure? What else can you expect?

Well, as Little Miss Always Turned My Homework In On Time, I'm a sucker for structure. As far as I'm concerned, life is messy and complicated and overwhelming at the best of times – as are those drawers in your mind that you're just now daring to open. As such, I have applied a format to this book that I hope will make the task of embracing your vulnerability and tackling these issues more doable, more digestible and more achievable.

Based on a mixture of my own experience, conversations with others – some experts in their field, some wise and willing to share their stories – and a knack for digging through some jargon-filled, hyperbolic research and teasing out the bits that can help us make sense of things, I have observed a series of issues or problems, if you will, that so many of us can relate to.

I would describe these issues more specifically as thought patterns, beliefs and, sometimes, behaviours in which I regularly engage that have certainly been affecting me negatively in recent years.

A desire to make a change but an inability to stick at it is one example. Our experience of imposter syndrome is another. Our fear that someone else's success would take from ours or the belief that everybody has to like us in order for us to be OK are two more.

In looking at these behaviours, I then dove head first into the pool of vulnerability, upon which I collated a series of 'truths'. These truths, which form the overall structure of the book, have been a game changer for me. From 'not everyone will like you' to 'you can do anything, but you can't do everything', *Naked* is a curation of the kind of blunt and uncomfortable truths you might not always want to hear, but the kind that will help you to course-correct when things get difficult. The dunk in the bitterly cold winter sea that you dread in advance but feel bloody brilliant about afterwards.

In some places, they go against the grain of popular discourse – such as my rejection of the concept of an 'end goal' – and, in others, they're what you already know to be true but perhaps need to be reminded of and, more importantly, need to start believing. They're what I need to be reminded of myself.

Some parts of this book are more 'gentle hug' while others are more 'kick up the arse', because, sometimes, we need a bit of both.

Let it also be said that you may already be familiar with a lot of the ideas put forward in this book; I'm not reinventing the wheel, per se, but I am taking the spokes apart and rearranging them in a way that makes the bike a little bit easier to ride.

I was already familiar with the reality that people-pleasing wasn't exactly doing me any favours, for example, but until I embarked on the project that became this book, it hadn't quite sunk in for me.

By bringing together these truths in what is often described as my trademark bullshit-free manner – if we're going to do all this work on ourselves we may as well have fun while we're doing it, right? – my hope is that at least one truth, if not all of them, will resonate with you to such an extent that it enables you to change whatever it is in your life that's been holding you back, causing you stress, giving you anxiety or wasting your time.

You'll notice that each truth, when explored, contradicts what I automatically believed or how I've been thinking and behaving. For example, I dive into why someone else's success doesn't take from mine because, at times (certainly until I got my head around it), I've been known to think, feel and behave as though it does, which obviously isn't a great way to be.

It impacts me negatively, adding to my anxiety and stifling my confidence. It slows me down on my own path and, quite frankly, it just makes me feel like a pile of pants.

Similarly, I stress the importance of failing in order to build resilience, which goes against my inherent perfectionist desire to get things right every single time.

With each chapter, I start by looking at how things are - why we might be feeling, thinking, reacting and behaving the way that we do - before offering the necessary truths, complete with practical action plans and advice where relevant. At the end of each chapter, you'll find a pause for thought, with which to gather yourself before moving on to the next topic. Then, together, we can take back ownership of our experience, pursue the change we're after and create the life we want.

The life where we are kinder to ourselves, where we don't get stuck in the daily rut of social comparison, where we worry less about what people think of us, where we feel content more often than not, where we have clarity, where we can appreciate and enjoy the journey without putting so much weight on the end result, and where we're no longer allergic to the idea of showing our vulnerability.

Lastly, a note on how to approach this book: I've structured *Naked* in such a way that each chapter, or 'truth', can stand on its own, meaning you can dip into the section that's most relevant to you at the moment you're reading it, but, of course, you can enjoy the book from beginning to end as well.

As with the books I read myself, even the Pulitzer-prize-winning ones, my advice to you is to always take the stuff that speaks to you and forget the rest. I promise I won't be offended. That being said, Chapter 2 - the truth about changing your life - is mandatory.

Now then, are you ready to get *Naked*?

Truth #1
You'll never have it
all figured out

THIS TRUTH IS SHORT and simple to whet your appetite: you'll never have it all figured out.

From the painstaking process of putting the first draft of this book together (the edit of which is always categorically woeful, though few writers want to admit this), right through to the final version which you are now reading, writing this book has, without a doubt, been the most self-doubt-riddling and vulnerability-inducing task of my professional life. The most self-doubt-riddling and vulnerability-inducing experience of my personal life? Coming home with my newborn baby, but that's another book entirely.

You see, when I began, I approached it all wrong: I put myself under a level of pressure that I would never be able to satisfy. I decided that after two bestselling books, I must have everything figured out if I'm to pen any sort of how-best-to-live-your-life guide. 'I should be an expert! I should be nailing this whole life thing!' I told myself, with the harsh, self-critical tone that I'd grown so used to hearing over the years.

The book would have to be a foolproof blueprint that any reader could implement and thus change their life forever. My words would have to leap off the page with the unquestionable assurance of someone like Oprah. 'I need to be like Oprah. WHY CAN'T I BE LIKE OPRAH!'

Needless to say, I was about an hour into day one of book-writing when I said to myself, 'Oh shit. Oh shit-fuck-shit-arse-wank-er-fuck. I can't do it.' I sent my editor a text saying much the same (she's cool like that), secretly hoping she'd tell me to just sack it off. One get-out-of-jail-free card for frauds, please? Because that's what I am: a fraud! And the moment I hand this manuscript over is the moment I'll be found out. Balls.

No sooner had the realisation of my own perceived inadequacy hit me than my old familiar friends 'anxiety' and 'imposter syndrome' swooped in, grabbed a drink and took a seat beside me. 'Hey, you. It's been a while,' they said, smug smirks on their faces.

With their presence, I felt instantly disrobed, exposed to the cellulite-speckled vulnerability that hid underneath (and, yes, perhaps a little bit crazy for personifying anxiety and imposter syndrome in the first place).

The anxiety I understood. It always had and always would present itself when something significant came along in my life, be it personal or professional, and I was no longer scared of it. In fact, if I didn't freak out before embarking on something that really matters to me, I'd be worried. That's just how I roll. That feeling of *Oh God, can I do this?* coupled with thoughts such as *Life would definitely be easier if I didn't take this on!* had become my own call to action. Anxiety in this instance was uncomfortable, yes, but it was also a useful tool that prepared me to face the task ahead, sharpening my senses and encouraging me to test the waters and see if I might come out the other side.

In situations like these, I had made my anxiety work in my favour. I needed it.

The imposter syndrome, however, was a little tougher to ignore. Was I really an imposter? Or was it just a narrative offered up to me by my vulnerable mindset that I chose to buy into?

From my understanding, imposter syndrome, which is experienced by at least 70 per cent of us at one point or another, comes in several forms. Most definitions focus on a person's inability to accept that the success they've achieved is really deserved. This is particularly common with women who, more so than men, tend to credit much of their success to luck or being-in-the-right-place-at-the-right-time rather than to the hard work and tenacity that they had shown to get them there.

Considered this way, imposter syndrome is a belief that you are fraudulent or a failure despite evidence to the contrary.

Having been given the opportunity to write my first book, I could definitely relate to this kind of imposter syndrome. Did I deserve the chance to write this? I didn't think so.

When the time came to put pen to paper for book number three, however, the imposter syndrome took on a slightly different form. At this point, it became the sinister-sounding name given to that very common feeling of dissonance we experience when we believe that what we put out to the world about ourselves is at odds with how we view ourselves privately. This is how I've most often experienced it. It's less about feeling like an imposter after you've achieved something, such as getting a promotion and feeling that you don't deserve it, and more about feeling like an imposter as you're about to embark on something or as you're right in the thick of it, such as feeling like an imposter during an interview when you are trying to come across as being more capable than you perhaps feel.

In this instance, what I had hoped to put out to the world at this stage of my writing career was that I was now a bona-fide expert. But, in reality, with no more letters after my name than I had the first time around and no more qualifications under my belt, my being an expert or not was not a matter of subjective opinion. I was not an expert.

More panic ensued. Should I accept this fact and pack it in?

Or should I proceed with my chest puffed, hoping that nobody calls me out on it?

I considered my options.

Had I decided to put it out there that I was an expert, continuing to write this book under the guise of having everything already figured out, my feelings of imposter syndrome would have been entirely justified and I'd have to deal with its presence, goading me all of the time. Not ideal. And I couldn't exactly abandon ship – I'd signed a contract. I did have a third option though. In order to forge ahead and save myself from this affliction, which you might argue is a very unhelpful side-effect of the fake-it-till-you-make-it don't-let-them-smell-your-fear rhetoric of the 1990s, I would have to somehow close the gap between how I was presenting myself and how I really was. To do that required vulnerability, which, as I sat down to write page one of chapter one, I wasn't all that ready to confront.

In response to my text, my editor laughed at me, saying, 'But you're writing a book that explores vulnerability; isn't that kind of the point? You're supposed to feel this way. The challenge for you will be pushing through that self-doubt and coming out the other side.'

I wasn't happy about it but, shit, she was right – feeling this way was a necessary, if sometimes torturous, part of the process. And not just with this book, but with life too.

It took me a while to accept it – and it's something I have to bring to my attention again and again – but here's the first truth I had to confront, the first pill I had to swallow: I will never have it all figured out. And the same is true for you.

We're never going to have all the answers to such a point that we never doubt ourselves. Not knowing is the plight of the human condition. But that's OK. In fact, it's more than OK – not knowing keeps things interesting. If we did have all the answers, life would be pretty boring. We wouldn't bother our arses moving forward to grow or to learn.

And so, in my attempt to remedy the dichotomy that gives rise to imposter syndrome, allow me to speak frankly and without exaggeration: I don't know any more about how to live life than you do.

Even doctors don't have it all figured out (though you'd certainly hope they'd know more than you as they approach you with a scalpel). What I do have to offer is this: I share my experiences – what I've learned and continue to learn about everything from confidence to anxiety, stress at work to happiness at home – through my writing. I don't start on page one with all the answers, though that would have been a much nicer process, of course. Instead, I'm figuring things out, in real time, as I type these very words.

While I may not be an expert in the traditional sense, I am curious. I have always been fascinated with how our minds work. How our thoughts influence our feelings and how our feelings influence our behaviours and how both of these impact our day-to-day lives.

I adore nothing more than reading about the neuroscience that sheds light on how and why we function the way that we do. While others are consumed by questions about what lies beyond this little planet of ours, I'm more concerned with what's happening with that pile of blubber inside our heads: the lumpy mass at the centre of everything we do, that despite weighing an average of three pounds, and representing a mere 2 per cent of an adult's body weight, requires 20 per cent, if not more, of our total body energy to do its job. It's the most demanding organ we have and though it looks like nothing more than a mound of minced meat (not that I've spent too long looking at brains in real life), it's home to over 100 billion neurons that communicate with each other all day long, enabling us to put one foot in front of the other and solve complex problems.

As someone who has experienced significant anxiety in her life thus far, and as a general overthinker and analyser extraordinaire, I'm always interested in understanding more about what makes us tick. Why? Because, for me, having that knowledge is the ultimate tool for empowerment. It's my greatest coping mechanism.

Granted, there will be times when no matter how much you think you have it sussed, life will come along and knock you sideways, but I'm curious about anything that helps me make sense of my experiences, anything that helps me to become more resilient and more able to handle the curve balls that life will inevitably throw our way. That way, I can bounce back to a state of relative contentment. By reading this book, I assume you are curious too.

Another, perhaps unfair, pressure I placed on myself was this: I am in my early thirties and, despite the introduction of fine lines around the eyes (and 'expressive' forehead folds in which I could probably hold a pencil), you could argue that I'm still relatively wet behind the ears. Do I know my arse from my elbow? Not yet, no. Shouldn't I wait until I'm at least fifty or the elusive age at which I will have everything figured out with years of worldly wisdom and experience in my rear-view mirror?

Well, no. Fuck that.

Because not even Oprah (God forgive me) or Tony Robbins (sorry, big fan of his work) or the person whose job it is to make all of the platitudes on Pinterest look pretty has it all figured out. You might spend a small fortune on motivational seminars and walk away with truckloads of inspiration and food for thought, but the truth is that not a single person on this planet has their shit together to such an extent that they can tell the rest of us how to live. Not me, not you, not the person whose perfectly curated Instagram makes you say, 'Oh, for fuck's sake', in mild annoyance.

There is no definitive guide to getting this right. Suffering, failure, mistakes, colossal cock-ups and falling flat on your face - these are all central tenets of the human condition that we will continue to experience right up until the day we pop our clogs.

We can't avoid it - and we shouldn't try to.

What we can do, though, is share our experiences, our learnings and our observations in an attempt to support each other. Together, we can draw conclusions that might make life a little bit easier to navigate. We can say, 'Oh, that actually makes sense' or 'Oh yeah, I guess I'm not the only person who feels like this', and, from there, we can be a little bit kinder to ourselves.

One thing we're really good at is connecting with other humans. I really see it as our greatest asset and, as we'll touch on in a later chapter, it is one of the most essential ingredients for happiness. But to allow for that connection and happiness, we need to allow ourselves to be vulnerable, which is what this book, in essence, is all about.

We all fall apart or maybe we just trip up from time to time, but then, with a bit of help, self-awareness and understanding, we try to put ourselves back together. But, again, in order to put ourselves back together, we need to allow ourselves to be vulnerable. Whether we're ten, twenty, fifty-five or we live to a hundred, we consistently learn and grow and stretch and crumble and strengthen and observe.

Like a muscle worked in the gym, we're always tearing and then rebuilding a stronger self.

We continually shapeshift through life, responding to the various experiences that come our way and the series of choices we make. And though I might only be the tender age of thirty-two at the time of this book's initial publication, there is no age restriction on wisdom, and certainly none when it comes to curiosity.

As Richard Templar wrote in *The Rules of Life*: 'You'll get older but not necessarily wiser', which is either comforting or worrying, depending on how you look at it.

I asked my mum if at her age – sixty-five – she now knew her arse from her elbow, which is an Irish way of saying that you know what you're doing or that you have it all figured out. Do you ever reach such a point?

Her answer was this. 'All I know is that one of them is bigger than the other.'

Suffice it to say she's a constant source of inspiration for me.

And so, after a long, head-banging-against-the-wall battle with the voice of imposter syndrome inside me that longed to roar about my inadequacies from the rooftops, I have arrived at the book you now hold in your hands. How did I win the war? By surrendering. By allowing for the fact that I'll never have it all figured out – by Googling incredibly accomplished people and discovering that, behind the scenes, they're just as clueless as the rest of us; by giving up on trying to be something I'm not; by stripping back the layers of pretence that we all long to hide behind; by not just accepting, but owning my vulnerability and sharing it with you; by getting real; and, ultimately, by getting – as the title of this book suggests – naked.

The thing is, try as we (writers) might, there is no single book that can solve the problems of the world, give you one neatly packaged recipe for happiness, cure you of all stress and anxiety so that you never have to experience it again, or help you find true and everlasting love (that might be Tinder you're thinking of).

There are only words put together, by people who are still figuring out their shit too (yes, even you with your fancy pants enlightenment, Eckhart Tolle, author of *The Power of Now*), in such a way that what is being said resonates with you because it mirrors what you're going through.

Words that make you feel less alone, like someone else just gets it. Words that give you the information you need, as well as the encouragement, to make a change or move forward. Words that give you a fresh perspective or a reassuring nudge in the right direction, and reflect what you know to be true but perhaps have forgotten or are afraid to admit. That's what I hope I've achieved with *Naked: Ten Truths To Change Your Life*. Ten observations, reminders and fresh perspectives that help you to understand why things are the way they are and why we do what we do, before enabling you to make the changes or adjustments necessary to your day-to-day experience that, over time, will have a major, positive impact on your life.

Shall we get stuck into something meatier now?

Great, but one thing first ...

 PAUSE FOR THOUGHT

Try to understand where your feelings of imposter syndrome stem from.

If it's the feeling that you are undeserving of what you have achieved, shift your attention towards the undisputed facts. Chances are, there was more than luck involved. If, like me, it's a fear that you don't have it all figured out, accept the truth that you never will – it's so freeing when you do – but don't let that stop you.

Ask questions, ask for help, voice your uncertainty confidently, safe in the knowledge that everybody else is either feeling the very same way or has done so in the past.

Find opportunities in your life to close the gap on your experience of imposter syndrome. Notice where there are significant gaps between how you put yourself out there to the world and how you really feel. Is it in a relationship? Is it at work? Can you bring these various versions of yourself closer together? When you close this gap and own your vulnerability in whichever situation you have imposter syndrome about, the imposter syndrome goes away. Trust me.

Not having all the answers right now doesn't make you any less capable of finding them out along the way.

Truth #2
There's nothing easy about changing your life

BEFORE WE DIVE into this chapter, allow me to preface it with the following clarification.

I'm not suggesting that you should or need to change your life. Maybe you don't want to change a single thing - that's bloody brilliant if you don't (and I'm a bit jealous). Maybe you were gifted this book, your bus is stuck in traffic, your phone battery is dead and you need something - anything - to read to pass the time. Totally fine. The hard copy also makes for a good coaster.

If you *do* want to change something about your life, however, that's OK too. You see, it doesn't have to come from a negative headspace, where we're just never happy with ourselves and there's always something that could be better. It can be a positive change that makes your life easier, such as, 'I want to start putting myself first more often' or 'changing this could minimise my stress and anxiety'. Less of the self-critical 'this is bad and this needs to change now' and more of the self-compassionate 'this could be better, for me'.

When we reframe change in this way, it becomes change that's *for* you rather than *against* you.

Another note: when I talk about change in this chapter – or throughout this book, for that matter – I'm referring to behavioural change. I would argue that it's our behaviours, which are informed by our thoughts and feelings, that largely determine the kind of life we live.

To begin, we must take a moment to unpack and reflect upon the truth about 'changing your life'. I find it helps to consider a quote from Robin Sharma, in his book *The 5 AM Club*, 'All truth is hard at the beginning, messy in the middle and gorgeous at the end.' Whether it's a little refining or a complete Brittany-Murphy's-character-in-*Clueless* overhaul, I'm going to assume that you've picked up this book with a dose of self-improvement in mind.

At one point or another – or as often as every week in my case – it's likely that you've thought about a behavioural change. 'I'd like to stop reacting this way', 'I wish I could stop saying yes to things I don't want to do', 'I need to care less about what people think of me', 'I really should stop eating mounds of chocolate because, to be quite honest, being lactose intolerant, it gives me diarrhoea' – well, maybe that last one's just me. If these kinds of thoughts are all too familiar to you, welcome to the club, membership is free.

As we are particularly hungry for change at the turn of a new year, and therefore more susceptible, we tend to fall victim to the idea that by reading one magical book (oh hi, *The Secret*) or watching one inspiring TED Talk, we'll instantly become new and improved versions of ourselves.

I for one have lost count of the number of motivational journals I've bought, firmly of the belief that this time, this journal (and not the previous eleven) will be the one to transform me into an organised queen who's always on top of her taxes and gets her exercise out of the way before breakfast. And how helpful have they actually been? Well, they certainly do a good job propping up the computer monitor to a more convenient eye level.

But it's not the journal's fault, it's me. I start with the best of intentions, recording everything from my water intake to my menstrual flow, noting how grateful I am for the little things like my morning bowl of porridge – or the joy of a good poo! – and then, after a few days, it all falls by the wayside and the journal assumes its lifelong role as something to plonk my cup of coffee on.

I've stared at motivational quotations long enough to be convinced that I've internalised them and therefore, the work is done: 'Thank you, Pinterest, I will never get stuck in a trap of social comparison again!'

By merely posting a quotation on Instagram (while under my duvet, of course), I've envisioned myself as a phoenix, rising from the ashes of my former unchanged self. 'New me, who dis?' Ahh, if only it were that simple.

Here's the thing (and this chapter's central truth): those of us who want to change our lives (but struggle to do so) want this change to happen instantly without us really having to change anything at all.

Think about it.

I'm brilliant at the not-changing-anything part. My agent, Amy, will attest to that. She's the best. She's kind and supportive, but she'll also tell me how it is. She's more of a mentor/life-coach/ therapist/bullshit-caller-outer than just an agent.

I remember meeting with her for one of our monthly catch-ups and saying that I wanted to do this and that. 'I want more of this!' and 'I'd like to get myself to this point!', bursting at the seams with enthusiasm.

She said, 'Great, off you go and set that in motion.'

I then came back to her a month later and repeated myself, 'Yeah, so, I still want to do this and that and get here.'

She stopped me and said, 'Caroline, your ideas are great. That you want to do these things is great. But what have you actually done about it? What are you doing to make these changes?'

Admittedly, it felt as though saying it and wanting it was enough, in the same way a new haul of gym clothes can feel like you're already there before you've even lifted a dumbbell.

If you're anything like me, you'll find that you get stuck in a gluey inertia between thinking about taking some kind of action and actually taking it.

The same goes for writing this book. For about six months, when people would ask me what I was up to workwise, I'd say, 'Oh I'm writing my third book.' I would also tell myself, and others, that my plan was to start getting up at 5 am every day – inspired by Robin Sharma (who certainly seems to have it all figured out, even if it's just an illusion) – so that I could get it written before my work day even began. Brilliant idea. However, when a friend checked back in months later and asked me how it was coming along, I realised that in the whole time I had been saying this, I hadn't written a tap. I hadn't even started it! And the only time I had gotten up at 5 am was with great difficulty and to catch a flight.

When I stopped berating myself for getting nowhere, which is never as self-motivating as we think it will be, I pondered what was driving my inaction. I realised that my slothfulness in these instances was partly born out of a fear of failure. Until you try something, it still has all of the potential to be great, right?

For the most part, though, I found it almost impossible to get going on the book because change of any kind is really fucking hard.

It takes time. It takes work. It takes stepping outside of your comfort zone. It takes stepping right into discomfort. It takes willpower (something that, as we'll get to in a moment, I completely misunderstood).

Making a real change requires that we take a long, hard look in the mirror at who we are, what we do and how we operate. We have to look at what's not working or what we're not doing – and that's not a very enjoyable exercise. Doing this puts us in a vulnerable position and we don't tend to like that.

Vulnerability = bad, or so we've been conditioned to believe.

And so, we just gloss over it. We toy with the idea of change, while continuing with the same cycle of behaviours, expecting different results.

For any positive change in your life to occur, I've learned that you need to start with the following two ingredients:

1 a willingness to be vulnerable, because you might feel uncomfortable and because you might fail;
2 an understanding of why change, even when you really want it, is hard.

Understanding the importance of the former is discussed more in Chapter 5, so, for now, we'll tackle the latter.

As Charles Duhigg so eloquently put it in his Pulitzer-prize-winning book *The Power of Habit*: '[T]he difference between who you are and who you want to be is what you do.'

It's not the books you read (apologies in advance to my publishers). This book is merely an aid to help you as you go about the change you want – but it can't actually do the work for you.

You might feel pumped and decide that you're going to wake up tomorrow and no longer be a victim of perpetual people-pleasing or that you're going to stop being so hard on yourself or that you're done with your habit of scrolling social media in bed. Unfortunately, though, it's never as easy as identifying something and then deciding to stop doing it.

It's been well established within psychology circles that the reason we find it so hard to make a change in our lives is because of our brain's tendency towards habits. Though we might not be aware of it, habits are at the source of almost everything we do and everything that goes on around us. And as Duhigg explains, it's only when we get clarity on what drives our behaviours that we can go about changing them.

As much as possible, our brains like to maintain homeostasis – in other words, they pretty much default to lazy.

We've evolved this way because the more we can do on autopilot, without really thinking about it, the more our brains can give energy to where it's really needed (e.g. solving a complex problem at work that requires intense focus). By letting things for the most part happen automatically, we give the prefrontal cortex – the higher-thinking, executive and rational part of our brain – a rest. When it works, it works really hard. In some ways, your prefrontal cortex is a bit of a diva; it does not want to be disturbed unless it's absolutely necessary. It's not getting out of bed unless it's really worth it.

The brain will always want to choose the path of least resistance and though that's supposed to be helpful from a conservation perspective, it doesn't always have our best interests in mind. Your brain will always say, 'What's the easiest thing to do right now that will keep me in my beloved state of equanimity?' For example, 'Eat the muffin right in front of me or make a salad from scratch?', 'Stay on the sofa or get up and do a workout?' – it doesn't give much thought to the bigger picture or how what we do now will impact our future selves. It doesn't want to wake up the prefrontal cortex so it weighs things up: can we just do this on autopilot? Can we do this without making an effort?·

Not only does our brain naturally want to keep us from overthinking everything we do (for example, it's just not a good use of our brain's resources to have to ponder every step of making a cup of tea every single morning), it also forms habits that make things easier for us (or rather, easier for *it* because, again, it's a bit lazy).

If you've ever felt stuck in a rut or a particular pattern of thinking or behaviour, it's because your brain has made a habit of it. Our brains form habits as a way of conserving energy.

The neuroscience of habits has been studied extensively and, for me, understanding the science is crucial when it comes to understanding why change is hard. Psychologist and economist Daniel Kahneman, author of *Thinking Fast and Slow*, explains this process in a particularly snackable way.

He refers to our prefrontal cortex – which, as you now know, is the part of our brain analysing the best course of action and making decisions, it's not really involved when it comes to performing habits – as 'System 2'. For an alternative characterisation, psychiatrist Steve Peters, author of *The Chimp Paradox*, refers to this part of our brain as the 'Adult'. The other part of our brain – the part that's more impulsive, that works on autopilot, carrying out habits almost unconsciously – is known to Kahneman as 'System 1', while others will refer to it as the primitive brain. Peters goes one step further and calls it the 'Chimp', which is pretty spot on in my opinion.

So you have System 1: the primitive brain, comprised of the hippocampus, amygdala and hypothalamus, which were among the first parts of our brain to develop back when surviving was really hard, and System 2: the adult brain, the prefrontal cortex, the part of our brain that developed much later on in our evolution. These two systems are sometimes in conflict – like angels and devils on our shoulders – especially when it comes to a test of our willpower, which we'll get to in just a moment.

The prefrontal cortex's job is usually to encourage the brain to do the right thing and, unfortunately, the right thing is often the hard thing; the primitive brain's job is to go straight for the easy option with little more than instant gratification and our survival in mind.

Let's think of a real-world example. When we're learning a new skill or starting a new routine, System 2 is called into action. We have to consciously think through every single thing we are doing. It's exhausting and it's effortful; we're analysing a lot of information and using lots of energy. Given that this is a disturbance to our brain's preferred homeostasis, it doesn't like this very much.

You'll be familiar with this if you've ever started a new job. In those first few weeks, you come home cognitively wiped out and ready for your PJs. But, when we do it day by day, week by week, the job gets easier. Eventually we do it without thinking too much; it requires less energy. This happens because we've sent the same message countless times from one part of our brain to another and, as a result, we've carved out a well-trodden path or, more specifically, a neural pathway.

When a neural pathway is set up and then repeated time and time again, it can run automatically when it is triggered. You get in the car, you stick the keys in the ignition and off you go without really thinking. You carry out your basic work tasks with something else on your mind. By this point, the work is handed over to System 1, your autopilot brain, freeing up your reserves once more. Your prefrontal cortex can resume its preferred slothful state.

This is primarily a good thing. If we had to give that much thought to our every move throughout the day, we would be worn out before lunch-time. That said, we can find ourselves developing neural pathways or habits that don't serve us all that well. Again, this is because our brain will pull us as much as possible towards what is easiest. For example, you'll notice that saying yes to someone's request for help in work is easier in the short term, even though your rational brain knows this will screw up your own workload later on. Our brain will gravitate towards what's easiest and then, over time, it'll start to set that course of action in stone.

So far, it seems our brains are pretty much hardwired to resist change - or, more specifically, change that's good for us - but that doesn't mean it's not possible, and it certainly shouldn't put you off. You can create new neural pathways and new habits that serve you well. To do this, you first need to become aware of our collective neurological predisposition towards resisting change. By merely understanding your behaviours, you're already on the way to changing them.

If you're still with me, that part's already done. Hurrah! Then, you're going to need to wrap your head around willpower. This one's a biggie.

Willpower is crucial for change, and understanding it is just as important. As with a huge number of our behaviours, such as people-pleasing and our tendency to focus on negative things, to understand why we have it, you have to go way back and look at willpower as a necessary ingredient for survival.

Hundreds of thousands of years ago, it was important that we had some ability to self-regulate, otherwise there would be a threat to our survival and we wouldn't have fared too well in our tribes. For example, back then, you had to go out and find your own source of food; you couldn't just sit back and then steal your neighbour's dinner. He or she would probably kill you in your sleep – and rightly so, they worked bloody hard to track down that wild beast. While that's unlikely to happen today – well, I have been known to have murderous thoughts upon realisation that somebody (my husband, namely) ate my last chicken nugget – it's served us well as we have evolved to continue exercising self-control.

Today, as research shows, willpower is linked with emotional resilience, greater life satisfaction, healthier relationships, better physical health – and even increased wealth.

One of the best-known studies on willpower is the 'marshmallow test' and was led by researcher Walter Mischel, now a psychologist with Columbia University. For his experiment, Mischel presented a group of toddlers with a plate of marshmallows. The kids were told that the adult in charge would have to leave the room for a short while and if they could wait until he returned, they could eat two marshmallows. If they couldn't wait, they could ring a bell, the adult would return, but, if they chose to do this, they would only be allowed to have one marshmallow. You can probably guess which option I'd have gone for.

Thirty years later, the researchers went back to the same kids to see how they were doing. As it turned out, the kids who had resisted temptation and exercised willpower seemed to be doing better than those who had not. They had better SAT scores – in fact their willpower was more a predictor of academic success than intelligence – and better BMI scores too, among other notable differences. This study showed, in a very simple way, the static impact that willpower can have on our lives.

Today, willpower is a word you'll hear a lot within the realm of self-improvement. It's what we rely on to accomplish every goal we set ourselves, big and small; with it, we can wake up our sleeping prefrontal cortex, and, when we do this, the primitive part of our brain is no longer in the driving seat of all that we do; the adult has arrived on the scene. With our willpower engaged, we can then create the habits that contribute towards the change we want.

We all have a vague idea about what willpower is and there are lots of definitions surrounding it – such as self-control, self-regulation, the ability to resist short-term temptations, the ability to override your primitive brain, the ability to choose long-term satisfaction over short-term gratification.

That said, willpower is thought of as something set in stone, like a personality trait. We look at someone who gets out of bed at 6 am every day for a workout class or who always gets their work done long before its due and think, *I wish I had your willpower.* I'm guilty of resigning myself to the idea that it's just not in my DNA, that I'll just never have the same ability to choose long-term satisfaction over short-term gratification. But this isn't true, *if* I work at it.

What doesn't appear to have been explored in the now-famous marshmallow study is the fact that the kids who couldn't resist temptation at the time could well have learned to do so over time, had they focused on developing their willpower. The study seemed to suggest that willpower was something that remained fixed in one group of kids and elusive in the other. To that, I call bullshit. While I may have been the kind of kid (or adult) who had a marshmallow in my mouth before they'd even finished explaining the process, that doesn't mean I'd be destined for a subpar life. I can make an effort to strengthen my willpower at any age, and so can you.

We are also largely unaware that willpower is something that, even when you're good at it, still needs nurturing and topping up regularly – you might say that even your willpower needs willpower. What's more, when you're tired or stressed out, your primitive brain will usually win the battle.

For a more granular understanding of willpower, I turned to Dr Kelly McGonigal, health psychologist and lecturer at Stanford University. (Sidenote: she also happens to be the woman from whom I learned that our perception of stress matters more than the presence of actual stress in our bodies, something I discussed in my first book, *Owning It*. Her book on the topic is called *The Upside of Stress*.)

In her 2011 book *The Willpower Instinct*, McGonigal breaks down willpower into three distinct aspects.

o 'I won't' power
o 'I will' power
o 'I want' power.

If there's one thing I struggle with, it's saying no to people. As I write this chapter, I'm in a sticky hotel room in Spain with no wifi and only crappy telenovelas on the TV. I needed to come here and cut myself off from temptation, excluding the occasional 'copa sangria', obviously. I needed to get away from all of the distractions of home in order to get this work done because whether it's my fridge humming at me to come and have a snack, my dog gazing at me with those big puppy eyes, my emails pinging or my Instagram feed that wants to show me how amazing someone else looks in a bikini, I just cannot, for love nor money, seem to say no. My 'I won't' power needs work, for sure.

'I won't' power is about saying no or choosing to opt out of something. For example, 'I won't eat that second bar of chocolate because I know I will feel sick' or 'I won't go to that event because I'll get home late and I really need an early night ahead of a busy day tomorrow'.

But, as McGonigal explains, there's more to willpower than saying no. It's not always about denying ourselves something. Sometimes, it's about taking positive action towards your goals or towards the change you want. This involves saying 'yes' or 'I will'. This is about opting in. She cites the example of staying on the treadmill for ten minutes longer than we want to as requiring 'I will' power. Or me saying, 'I will go to Spain to get some work done because that is what's best for me'.

Are you noticing the difference? When considered this way, willpower becomes something to work with instead of against.

The third aspect, then, is 'I want' power. It's less reactive and less immediate than 'I will' or 'I won't' power, which we call upon for guidance as we face various obstacles and triggers throughout our day. Instead, 'I want' power is the ability to go through our days with an overarching awareness of what contributes towards, and what detracts from, our goals, as well as the kind of life we want to live.

In general, 'I want' power helps to drive behaviours that are more in line with our values and the change we're after. Why? It's worth repeating Charles Duhigg's words once more: 'The difference between who you are and who you want to be is what you do.'

How to strengthen your willpower

Familiarise yourself with the following six steps for strengthening your willpower and you'll find yourself with a new advantage. The change you're after – the positive changes in mindset and behaviours that we're going to explore throughout this book – will be less elusive and more achievable than when we started out.

1. Reframe it

Refreshingly, McGonigal suggests that we focus as much as we can on the 'I want' aspect of willpower. She notes that, in the research that demonstrates that willpower is a limited resource and something that runs out, the focus is almost always centred on the participants' will to do things they don't want to do or that they don't care about, such as leaving your hand in a bucket of ice for as long as possible (which is a fun experiment, I'm sure, but not exactly something we really need to be doing in the real world, unless you're going to give me a large sum of money to see how long I can last).

However, the willpower that's required to do the things that we are passionate about, that will help contribute towards something that's important to us, is a lot less limited than we might have thought. To get more gas out of our willpower, she suggests that when we make a healthy-food choice, for example, over a not-so-healthy one, we reframe it in our minds as 'I want' or 'I will' power rather than the 'I won't' power of trying to resist the triple-cooked chips and deep-fried chicken balls of your local Chinese takeaway.

This is far more empowering than always thinking of your willpower as a tool for resistance and something you have to fight against. It swaps the very common 'deprivation mentality' that McGonigal speaks of and puts you in the driving seat, reimagining willpower as a tool for choice and positive change. This doesn't mean it won't be hard, but it might be a little bit easier.

In short, try to think of what you are saying yes to, rather than what you are saying no to. On a more macro level, have a clear idea of what you want for your life.

2. Get mindful

When we understand the psychology behind habits and willpower, it's time to take action. According to Charles Duhigg, the best place to start is with what he calls a 'cornerstone habit' and I've found this incredibly helpful.

A cornerstone habit is one that doesn't function in isolation. Instead, it's a habit that will have a positive knock-on effect in several other areas of your life. For one person, it could be going to the gym, which might then encourage them to eat healthier and procrastinate less.

Before we get that ambitious, though, I suggest you choose mindfulness. Why? Aside from all of the scientific proof that confirms how powerful mindfulness and meditation can be, if you prioritise the habit of increasing your self-awareness, you'll be far more tuned in to the willpower challenges you face each day.

Remember, so much of what we do happens on autopilot. If we can become more aware of the things we do on autopilot that don't serve us well, we can choose to engage our willpower, and let it inform our actions and behaviour. Of course, it's hard to suddenly just become more self-aware – your brain won't like it, remember – and it's also a bit of a vague suggestion, so make it more tangible by choosing to have a three-to-five-minute timeout for mindfulness each day; this will help to improve your awareness elsewhere too.

A guided meditation via one of the many apps available is your best bet. My favourite app is MyLife. Another option is to set an alarm on your phone and when it goes off, you continue with whatever you are doing (it doesn't have to interrupt you or require timeout) but you also become more aware of your surroundings, your activities, your thoughts and your body.

The more self-aware we become, the stronger our willpower gets and the easier it will be to apply it elsewhere.

3. Eat, sleep, move – prioritise the basics

As you will know from first-hand experience, being worn out physically and mentally is not your willpower's best friend. This makes sense, because to engage our prefrontal cortex, we need energy. We need to be firing on all cylinders for it to do its job. When we're exhausted, it becomes temporarily damaged.

When we've really been burning the candle at both ends, we suffer what's known as 'mild prefrontal dysfunction', which is where our brain struggles to regulate our emotions and our attention. When this happens, the primitive brain gets back in the driving seat, guiding us towards instant gratification and leading with emotion.

Of course, it's not possible to have full batteries all the time, so, when you don't, just understand that your willpower is compromised and don't be too hard on yourself. Prioritise your sleep and get over the ridiculous idea that you'll achieve more on less sleep – science has proven time and time again that this is bullshit. Sleep is your greatest asset when it comes to success in all areas of your life.

Then, I find it helps to start training your focus onto your future self, which McGonigal explains is a version of ourselves with whom we need to get familiar in order to strengthen our willpower at times when it's lacking. She says that, as humans, we have a far easier time looking back and recognising who we have been than looking forward and recognising who we will be, which makes sense because we've already lived those experiences. She contends that if we can look forward and create what she describes as a vivid 'self-defining future memory' of something that is going to feel important to us, such as imagining yourself experiencing a day where you haven't put your own needs at the bottom of your priority list, then that will further motivate our willpower.

Again, choose the self-compassionate approach of 'I'm doing this now for my future self', even if it's just making a mental note of what you will do when your energy is restored.

This is smart troubleshooting when your energy is low. For me, I know that my energy falls off towards the end of the day and I'm rarely up for much. This is why I don't exercise at night, I'll do it in the morning after I've had a good sleep and I find it a lot less effort to get myself to the gym. This is also why I will never allow myself to send an important email in the evening if I'm particularly exhausted. That is a time when my prefrontal cortex has left the party and my emotions are inflated. I can't really trust that I'm making the best choices – this is why you'll hear the phrase 'sleep on it' when it comes to important decisions or actions.

To keep your willpower reserves at a nice level, maintaining a solid sleep routine is hugely important. We know sleep is essential for almost every biochemical and psychological process in the mind and body – this is one of the reasons why a lack of sleep has been used as a form of torture – and so it goes without saying that sleep is crucial for willpower. You charge your willpower batteries while you sleep.

You'll notice this by how much easier it is to choose a healthier breakfast than it is to resist a late-night snack. Just as sleep is important, so too is your nourishment and your exercise. When I'm hangry (which is kind of my middle name), my willpower doesn't stand a chance. Exercise and good food can, for a lot of us, require willpower but they also serve as tools to stimulate willpower. Exercise, in particular, is another cornerstone habit that spreads out into other areas of our life.

While these are all healthy habits to develop in and of themselves, they're relevant here because they will help to strengthen your willpower. They give your prefrontal cortex the fuel it needs to wake up. To engage your willpower the next time you want to get up and exercise, remind yourself that you will get more willpower in return.

4. Tune into your energy's checks and balances

Another thing I find it helpful to be mindful of is my cognitive energy's checks and balances, particularly when I'm in that initial phase of carving out a new pathway for whatever change I'm trying to put in place.

If we know that trying to make a change takes a lot of mental effort and that our willpower is a finite resource, it would certainly make sense to me to try and conserve energy elsewhere. A good example here would be this: say you want to start going to the gym before work. But you also want to make a protein-filled smoothie to drink right after your workout. And then you have to also get yourself sorted for going to work straight from the gym, choosing your clothes, etc. That's a lot of willpower required at once. Automating the routine as much as you can makes this easier on yourself. The goal here is that when you get up in the morning, you're only calling on your willpower to get you to the gym – maybe even just to get your gym shoes on. Willpower used on anything else will be a drain. As such, leave out your gym clothes and your work clothes the night before and make sure that you have all the ingredients ready to lash into your blender (and, yes, that will require willpower the night before but when your sleepy brain argues with you that it will just do it in the morning, tell it, 'I'm doing this now to help my future self' and consider it a strategic brain hack). Granted, this all sounds incredibly simplistic, and, no, it's not a revolutionary idea, but I'm interested in how it helps to enable the change we want.

By automating our routine, it takes our prefrontal cortex out of the equation – we hand things as much as possible over to System 1. We don't have to engage our prefrontal cortex to make decisions in the morning about what to wear and what to eat. It cuts out what's known as 'decision fatigue', saving on cognitive resources so that we can then draw on them to get our ass to the gym. We conserve energy where possible so we can use it most effectively where it's needed. This is another reason why you're better off starting with small changes that build towards something than trying to transform yourself all at once. You'll likely struggle to make it all happen because there's just not enough willpower to go around.

Get a clear picture of what you'd like to achieve that's going to require willpower. Look for opportunities to automate your actions where possible – where can you conserve your willpower so that you can put it to better use? Lean into your willpower, for sure, but do not keep yourself in a constant state of willpower depletion.

5. Be realistic about your timeframe

You then need to accept the reality that change doesn't happen overnight. Or with just one profound tweet. Neural pathways have to be carved out over time, like a muscle in the gym. Lots and lots of repetition.

There's much debate around the length of time required to create a new habit or how long it takes for something to stick. Of course, it depends on a few things: what you're trying to change or implement, the circumstances, the kind of person that you are, whether or not it's something you can do daily, and so on and so forth. In my experience, three months or thereabouts is a good gauge with which to align your expectations.

For years, based on the word of Dr Maxwell Maltz (who sold over 30 million copies of *Psycho Cybernetics*, his 1960 book on behavioural change), it was believed that a mere twenty-one days was all that was needed for lasting change to occur, before old pathways would dissolve and new ones would begin to gel. Explained by James Clear, author of *Atomic Habits*, this idea stuck because twenty-one days was short enough to be inspiring and motivating (in other words, you'd be convinced to bother your arse) but still long enough to be believable. Unfortunately, though, this attractive promise of 'three weeks to a new you' was more of an observation of Maltz's than actually being based on science.

Decades later, Phillippa Lally, health psychology researcher at University College London, and her colleagues carried out a more comprehensive study to get clarity on how long it really takes for change to occur. Their study examined the habits of ninety-six people over a twelve-week timeframe. Each participant chose one new habit to implement over the course of three months, and had to report each day on whether or not they did the activity and if or when the activity started to feel automatic, thus becoming a habit.

For the purposes of this study, Lally and her colleagues chose basic changes, such as drinking a bottle of water with lunch or going for a fifteen-minute run. The researchers then analysed the data and arrived at the following conclusion: on average it took two months for a new behaviour to become automatic, sixty-six days to be exact. That being said, for some people, their change became automatic after as little as eighteen days, while, for others, it took 254 days. Again, it depends on the complexity of the habit. It's easy to measure how much caffeine you drink per day. It's less so to measure that you are becoming more compassionate with yourself. Some changes are more tangible than others.

What they also found was that 'missing one opportunity to perform the behaviour did not materially affect the habit formation process', which I would take as a gentle reminder not to harangue yourself if you have an off day. We are going to mess up now and then but, in general, if we are building towards habits that serve us well, without being discouraged by the fact that it might take longer than expected, we will eventually form those new neural pathways. It's not about the days, it's about the pattern.

We need to remember that being tired and stressed out is a major drain on our willpower resources and until we've passed the point where something has become automatic, where our System 2 has handed over the reins to our System 1, we'll likely hit some roadblocks.

6. Think small

Dr Sam Collins, author, motivational speaker and founder of Aspire (a global organisation empowering women in leadership), whom I interviewed for this book, is an advocate of thinking small. Granted, this doesn't sound super-uplifting but hear us out. We live in a world where we're constantly encouraged to think big and reach for the stars. Collins finds this unrealistic, and so do I. It's not about limiting your potential, it's about making things as easy on yourself as possible, so that your brain will work with you.

Think about all the times you've sat there, thinking big, and how often that's actually worked out for you. Too often, we bite off more than we can chew and it's too much of a leap for our habitual, stuck-in-its-ways brain. It's too much for our willpower, which needs gentle coaxing. And, as a result, we find ourselves in that state of inertia I mentioned earlier in this chapter.

For change to happen, and for your willpower to be given any sort of a chance to develop and grow, you need to embrace the idea of thinking small. Think teeny-tiny, even. For example, if you decide that, from tomorrow, you're never going to eat sugar again, your willpower might get you through the first day, but, by day two or three, you'll notice it's gone MIA, and you're likely to fail (this also has something to do with the addictive nature of sugar and its effect on your hormones, but the point still stands). If you decide instead that for one of your snacks each day you're going to have a piece of fruit rather than go cold turkey, your willpower will slowly and steadily get on board. You'll gently carve out a new neural pathway that eventually sees the healthier option as your default - and when that happens, you'll no longer need willpower to execute it, freeing up your willpower to take you to the next step.

In Chapter 6 I talk about one tiny change I made that made an enormous difference to my people-pleasing tendencies. Again, thinking small and taking smaller steps with minor adjustments to your behaviours will keep you from reaching that point of total willpower depletion.

What to expect when you're expecting change ...

Charles Duhigg, referenced thus far and considered the godfather of habit neuroscience, states emphatically that habits cannot be got rid of - they can only be altered or replaced - though new habits can be created.

At the core of each and every habit, according to MIT researchers referenced in Duhigg's *The Power of Habit*, you'll find a simple neurological loop made up of three elements.

1 There's a trigger or cue - the thing that makes you then execute the behaviour.

2 There's the behaviour or routine itself – the thing you do when triggered, and it is this part of a bad habit that you'll want to change.

3 There is the reward, which is what we get when we've completed the behaviour – it satisfies a craving, which may be something as straightforward as a sugar craving or it might be a craving you have to please others.

Duhigg cites a basic example. Each day he gets up from his desk, walks to the cafeteria and eats a chocolate muffin. This is the routine – the behaviour – that he wants to change. To do that, he must identify the cue that triggers the behaviour and understand the reward he gets from executing this behaviour. The cue might be hunger or boredom or that, at the same time each day, he feels the need for a break. The reward is the feeling of comfort and satisfaction he gets from eating the muffin. He feels temporarily good. But here's the thing: he's still going to find himself triggered by this cue and he's still going to crave this reward. He can't live a life hiding away from triggers and cues. But with willpower, he is able to change the middle part of this routine, which is the behaviour.

This is what he calls the 'Golden Rule of Habits', keeping the same cue and reward but changing the routine for whatever it is we're trying to improve in our lives. He applies this framework to habits that are arguably more straightforward, where it will be easier to identify each of the three steps. It'll likely be more tangible, and something you can see yourself doing every day. When it comes to behaviours such as people-pleasing however, it's a little bit more complicated.

The three stages of making a lasting change

Whether you're trying to become more organised by getting up earlier or you want to be less hard on yourself or become less of an incessant people-pleaser or want to implement a more regular exercise regimen, you need to be aware of what to expect.

We have covered the average timeframe for installing new habits, settling on the realistic number of sixty-six days, assuming it's something you can do every day (you might not be confronted with your people-pleasing habit every single day). With those sixty-six days, I want to bring you back to the quotation that started us off at the beginning of this chapter. 'All truth is hard at the beginning, messy in the middle and gorgeous at the end.' With this eloquent quotation, the person who said it – Robin Sharma – is referring to three distinct stages of making a change, which we can divide into three twenty-two-day chunks.

As outlined in his book *The 5 AM Club*, where he encourages readers, very convincingly, to begin every single day at 5 am, the three distinct stages are as follows:

1 destruction
2 implementation
3 integration.

The first chunk – destruction – is the hardest phase. Needless to say, it's not fun. You're met with a lot of resistance from your brain who, as we know, is not on board with this whole changing business. You're going to feel like packing it in. You're letting go of an old routine and old thinking patterns and you'll probably mess up (which is OK). In relation to the 5 am wake-up time, this is going to feel like torture. You're going to be drawing heavily on your 'I Won't' power.

The second chunk – implementation – is still pretty hard but, at this point, something is happening. During this phase, your neuro-architecture changes; you're no longer met with a brick wall where no neural pathway exists, you have begun the process of carving out a neural pathway that supports your new behaviour. It's not a free-flowing river yet but you're walking down the pathway and taking in your new surroundings. As per his original quotation, it's a tad messy but you remind yourself why this is important to you; you recruit your 'I Will' power and your 'I Want' power. At this point, you've done the hardest work.

When you enter the final twenty-two days – integration – you're incorporating your new behaviour into your psychological fabric. This is where you are automating the change you've made so that it no longer requires willpower or the help of your prefrontal cortex.

What was incredibly difficult at the beginning is now less so. If you've ever persevered when going from zero to three gym sessions per week, you'll recognise each of these three phases. Don't expect to skip the first two and go straight to the good bit, remember that change is meant to be hard.

 PAUSE FOR THOUGHT

We don't like hearing it but the truth about change is that it's not easy. Not at all. But it's not because you're lazy or because you alone are bad at it, it's difficult for all humans to make a change. The good news is it is doable.

Now that we understand what's required to make a change in our lives – be it a thinking or behavioural pattern that's not serving us very well – we can move on to look at some of the changes we've probably been turning a blind eye to but that we'd ultimately like to address. There may be changes you're already thinking of that would make a big difference in your life.

The following chapters look at some of the necessary changes I've tried to make across my thoughts, beliefs and behaviours – there's a lot that I'm still in the process of changing so remember, I'm right there with you. You may find that you can relate to a good many if not all of them.

Next on the agenda, truth number three: You can do anything but you can't do everything. Time to tackle our tendency towards burnout.

Truth #3
You can do anything, but you can't do everything

IT'S FAIR TO SAY that this is the first generation of women to have it all – or to at least strive to have it all. While there's a whole other conversation to be had around gender equality, which still has a long way to go, when you compare our mothers' and grandmothers' experience with that of women today (particularly those falling within the millennial bracket), we now have considerably more opportunities available to us.

We're told to dream big and reach for the stars – and, consequently, we have a lot more choices to make. And it's wonderful! We can do anything we set our minds to! *Punches the air/ unfastens bra.*

It's not assumed that we should stay at home all day, vacuuming and chopping carrots, but we can if that's what makes us happy. We can be – and most of us want to be – financially independent. We're living longer than ever before and we're healthier too. We don't have to get married for security; we can marry someone, on equal terms, for love. If we do marry, we won't have to give up our job. We aren't expected to have kids or at least to have popped them out before we've hit the big three-oh (which, on a side note, no longer signifies the demise of our youth). We can have kids and work. We can have kids and not work. We can work and not have kids. We can travel. We can continue educating ourselves. We can be as career-focused as we want to be.

It's all very exciting and the possibilities seem endless. And so, perhaps to honour the generations of women who have gone before us, who didn't have these same choices, we go for it all. We go for the high grades, the top college course, the internship, the part-time job, the year around the world, the full-time job, the part-time master's degree while we work the full-time job, the partner, the marriage, the balanced diet, the rich social life, the Tuesday-night tag rugby team, the Thursday-night book club, the 6 am yoga class, the personal trainer, the child, the house, the promotion, the spare to your heir, the extension, the city break with the girls and the romantic getaway with the other half – and don't forget the constant healthy meal prep, the counting of micros and macros and, of course, the side hustle/passion project on which you can unleash your inner creativity. Oh, and the carefully curated social media presence that's equal parts funny, relatable and aspirational.

If you need a lie down, or a stiff drink, just reading that, you're not alone.

The thing is, we don't just want to simply *do* any and all of these things, we want to *nail* them. We want to do everything, do it perfectly, and do it now.

I've observed not just with my own experience but with lots of the women who surround me (and, yes, it is unequivocally harder for women than men, especially if kids are on the table, because it is the female of the species who has to grow and then eject the watermelon-sized human from the narrow canal of her nether regions, dealing with the physical and emotional upheaval that goes along with it) the following correlation: ticking all of the aforementioned boxes comes at quite a cost, and usually that cost is ourselves.

Think about the various verticals that make up the priorities of your own life for a minute. Very rarely on that picture do we make time for ourselves, time to just breathe, time to just be. If we do, we feel guilty about it. We feel lazy. We think we really should be doing something else with our time. Something useful.

Here's a thought: downtime is useful. It's productive. Sometimes, it's the most productive thing you can do. The idea that it's wasteful is toxic. We give out to ourselves for taking it and then the guilt we place upon ourselves renders the break we've taken utterly pointless. So, we go back to spinning plates because we're comfortable with that.

It sounds good to be busy. We wear busy like a badge of honour and we want to prove to the world that despite what history has said of women, we can work just as hard, be taken just as seriously and be just as useful in the workplace as men. But with all of those plates spinning at any one time, you can be guaranteed that one will drop and the plate that tends to drop is our own well-being.

And I don't mean the well-being that you service at the gym or in your excruciating hot-yoga class or in the meeting room – these are all still to-dos on the never-ending list of to-dos. I'm talking about the well-being that gives you the space to take your foot off the pedal. To throw the to-do list to one side without guilt. The well-being that lets you leave the cups and the crumbs on the kitchen counter for another hour. The well-being that isn't about ticking every box so that you can feel you're 'winning at life' but is about having room to go slow. Where there's room for a 'you' day, even a 'you' five minutes. The well-being that has a good night's sleep at the top of your list.

Typically, when we fill our hours, days, weeks and months with all of the opportunities we now have access to, our own needs get relegated to the bottom of the list. And after a while, though we may not even realise it's happened, it seems we've pushed ourselves too far. We've taken on too much. We've drained the gas from our tank. While the benefits of all these opportunities and choices are obvious, the downside is that we struggle to tell what's important from what's not, and we experience decision fatigue. We keep at it for too long, and then we experience chronic stress and anxiety and maybe even panic attacks, which we think have come out of the blue but they have not.

This is when our sleep suffers, which then has a knock-on effect on everything from our immune system to our mental health to the productivity we've come to value so much. This is when we start to berate ourselves for not being able to do all of the things and be all things to all people. This is when we hit breaking point or step right onto the hot coals of burnout. Social media may tell a different story, but it's happening all around you, that I know for sure.

Burnout is something you'll definitely be familiar with even if you haven't personally experienced it. The term was first coined in 1974 by Herbert Freudenberger and it's been a buzzword for being overworked and overtired ever since. But it was only in the summer of 2019 that the World Health Organization finally acknowledged it as a psychological condition with a medical diagnosis, relevant to the workplace.

Essentially, it's a condition you're likely to face if chronic work-related stress is left unaddressed and unmanaged.

Burnout is different to stress in that it's not merely about struggling to cope with pressure or about feeling tired, it's about the physical sense that you're running on empty – that you're energy output is far greater than your energy input. You've lost all sense of your inner checks and balances. You're not able to function as normal. The most basic of tasks feels insurmountable. Your resilience has been depleted. Your immunity might be noticeably compromised and you'll come to the conclusion that you can no longer cope.

The World Health Organization stipulates that 'burnout refers specifically to phenomena in the occupational context, and should not be applied to describe experiences in other areas of life', but I would argue that these 'other areas' of our lives, where there's plenty of stress and endless to-do lists, certainly add more fuel to the burnout fire. For some people, it may only relate to work but, for a good many of us, it's a culmination of many things.

Today, burnout is being taken more seriously. We're slowly but surely moving away from a time when being completely flattened was something to boast about. Arianna Huffington, founder of The Huffington Post and author of *Thrive*, has been instrumental in this slow but steady societal shift. She successfully turned the heads of both workers and companies when she wrote about her story of burnout that saw her collapse to the floor from sleep deprivation and exhaustion, resulting in a broken cheekbone and a stint at the hospital. It wasn't until she had this major wake-up call that she realised enough was enough, that while she can probably do anything she puts her mind to, she cannot do everything. And that's OK.

Burnout is no longer the reserve of accomplished CEOs like Arianna Huffington or those run ragged on Wall Street. It's increasing at an alarming rate (according to recent findings reported by Forbes) and is experienced by men and women from all walks of life.

Huffington shared her story with the aim of warding people off getting to the point of collapse that she reached. Similarly, when I talk about my experience of crippling anxiety, which was the result of my own burnout, my goal is to help people recognise when they're heading towards the proverbial cliff edge, long before they fall off it.

Unfortunately though, from the conversations I have and the stories I read about those who now prioritise their self-care, it seems to be something we only begin to do or take seriously after we've reached that point of burnout. After we've had that wake-up call.

But you shouldn't have to smash your cheekbone into the ground or count ten panic attacks in one day in order to realise how important it is to look after yourself. Think of a car: you don't wait until you've broken down on the side of the road, with no petrol in your tank, before you think, *Oh maybe I should fill up*. We keep it topped up. We certainly fill the tank before we take a long road trip. Similarly, looking after ourselves shouldn't be something we do as a form of crisis management, when the shit has hit the fan; instead, it should be how we approach life, be it at work, at home or anywhere.

Here's a truth I'm no longer afraid to admit, and one that's improved my enjoyment of life tenfold: You can do anything, but you can't do everything.

Well, you can, technically, but, if you do, you're probably going to suffer. So, you need to decide what's worth it and be unapologetically ruthless about what's not. Plain and simple. Otherwise, you'll inevitably find that one of the things you're doing will give way, and chances are – if recent findings on 'burnout' are anything to go by – the thing that gives way will be you. Maybe you're already there. That's OK. If you are, or you sense that you're dancing on that fine line between coping and not coping, consider this chapter the life raft you've been looking for.

When you get close to, or reach, the point of burnout, changing the lifestyle factors that are causing it will obviously make a huge difference. You need to be brave and look at its root cause rather than just slapping a yoga class onto the end of your day to manage your stress. If we move beyond the individual, it's clear that an awful lot needs to happen from the top down in professional environments to look at why this is happening in the first place and ensure it's a trend that's curbed.

Arianna Huffington made yet another convincing plea to the corporate world in a recent address for Thrive Global. She said, 'Now, with burnout in the spotlight, companies have a fresh opportunity to step up, for the sake of their people and for the health of the bottom line. Focusing on people's actual experience at work is no longer a nice-to-have, it's a must-have for anyone who wants to succeed in the long run. To find the cure to "civilization's disease", it's going to take a commitment to getting to the root causes of burnout.'

To keep things in check, at an individual daily level, we need to look at what's not working for us and then confidently get the shearing scissors out. This requires adopting an essentialist mindset – and it's incredibly liberating – which we'll get to in just a moment. We can also switch on our inner amber light, something that will be explained in Chapter 9.

In the meantime, there are two crucial things we need to prioritise and make room for in our lives starting right now: self-compassion and sleep. The two Super Ss.

We'll look at self-compassion first.

Of all the things society has encouraged us to strive for, those things that we dig deep to find motivation to achieve, one thing we forget is self-compassion. Think about it: today's woman is strong, resilient, powerful, inspired, motivated but is she compassionate with herself? Is she gentle with or kind to herself? Not so much. It's for this, I believe, that we have to dig the deepest.

Self-compassion is something I've consciously pushed right up to the top of my priority list since realising, over time, that being too hard on myself and expecting too much of myself is a common thread at the centre of every roadblock I've come up against.

I'll share a recent example with you.

You may or may not be familiar with my anxiety story. In short, I went from living my life from one panic attack to the next for over a year – brought about by merely having too much going on in my life at once and a work environment that didn't work well with me – to managing my anxiety so that it doesn't manage me. The book about my experience, *Owning It* – and its podcast counterpart – did incredibly well and, soon enough, I was on the receiving end of hundreds of messages a week from people who had read the book and wanted to tell me about their own anxiety stories, as well as how much the book, which offers a practical blueprint for owning anxiety, helped them move past it.

Though I consistently stress the fact that I am not an expert on anxiety in the traditional sense, magazine features about the book have often referred to me as a 'millennial anxiety guru' among other things. Naturally, they were just looking for a catchy strapline to attract attention, and I was flattered, but the pressure to live up to the book's success started to seep in, and when I tried to get under the belly of *that* pressure, I realised that most of it was coming from me.

Even though I would openly say, 'Look, I still sometimes feel anxiety, I still have my wobbles', I started to believe that I had really outsmarted it, that I couldn't possibly experience bad anxiety again because I had written *the* book on it. I was now the person who people turned to – and, of course, that was far too much to expect of myself.

It was only a matter of time. In fact, as I write this chapter, I feel I am only now coming out the other side of it – I got my ass kicked by anxiety again. I wasn't expecting it, but I wasn't doing the work necessary to keep it in check (again, because I thought I was just beyond it) and for whatever combination of reasons, which I call vulnerability factors, I found myself, once again, feeling the anxiety I had worked so hard to distance myself from.

I find it's always helpful to be aware of what vulnerability factors are at play in your life, whenever you feel an increase in feelings of stress, being overwhelmed or anxious. Vulnerability factors are also relevant when we feel unusually irritable or angry.

The simplest example of a vulnerability factor would be something we're all familiar with: hangriness. When our body lacks the energy it needs to function, we become more vulnerable to erratic emotions. Another example could be when we don't get enough sleep and find that the following day we don't perform at the same level that we would have if we had received the appropriate amount of rest.

Some common vulnerability factors of my own have been the following:

• If I have been physically unwell, my ability to think positively is compromised.
• If I have been taking too much on, I notice myself getting snappier.

- If I have horrendous period pains, I'm more vulnerable to crying at an advert on television that really shouldn't incite tears.

Think about the vulnerability factors that might be having an effect on you. When you become aware of them, they can help to explain a lot, enabling a more measured and compassionate perspective as well as helping you to move past the issue more quickly.

It wasn't anxiety about an upcoming event, which I regularly experience and can totally handle because it comes and it goes, it was a constant sense of uneasiness and fear that just hung in my limbs from morning until night.

I swiftly freaked the fuck out (complete with Alice Cooper-style mascara dribbling down my cheeks). I swooped in like a first responder to assess the situation and put in place the tools and techniques I often write about. No sugar! No caffeine! No stress! I felt threatened by the anxiety, and so I went on the attack. I also expected that with one quick conversation, I'd be able to nip it in the bud. If I couldn't snap out of this then I'm clearly no anxiety 'guru'.

I hadn't felt it like that in about four years, so to feel it again really threw me. I blamed myself. I berated myself for not being able to think myself out of it.

'I should know better.'

'I should be able to.'

Then I realised the tools and techniques I had always relied upon weren't really working, and I freaked out some more, which served only to perpetuate the anxiety and the negative self-talk.

Eventually it hit me: the reason the tools weren't working was because I was lacking the most crucial ingredient of all: self-compassion. Without this, there's no amount of self-care in the world that's going to make a difference. I was devoid of the kind of compassion for myself that I would absolutely have shown to a friend. Only when I started to comfort myself – and really mean it – and turn down the volume of the drill sergeant inside my head, pressuring me to get my shit together, while turning up the volume on the more gentle side of myself, did I start to feel the anxiety lift.

Whereas a few days earlier, I would have been telling myself, 'This is ridiculous, you've handled way worse than this, get a grip', I was now beginning to say things like:

'You're doing your best.'

'You've had a lot on.'

'You can feel anxiety and still be supportive, via your work, to others dealing with anxiety.'

'Having a hard time with anxiety, despite having written a book about how to handle anxiety, does not mean you are a fraud.'

'You're doing fine.'

'You can pare things back for a few days, that's OK.'

'You say this so often but you don't hear it enough: it really is OK to not feel OK, even for you.'

The science of self-compassion

For a steer on what self-compassion is, how it impacts the brain and body, why it's important, and how to incorporate more of it into your life, you need look no further than researcher and bestselling author Dr Kristin Neff, Associate Professor at the University of Texas.

Neff was the first person to measure and operationally define the whole concept of 'self-compassion'. Where Brené Brown has centred her life's work around vulnerability and shame, for the brilliant Neff, it's all about self-kindness. For her, if you are your own worst enemy, then self-compassion is something you're probably lacking and something you should absolutely invest in.

She also believes that self-compassion is arguably more important than self-esteem. For self-esteem, we are looking for ways to see ourselves in a good light – perhaps in contrast to others – in order to feel worthy. She says self-esteem is dependent on things working out and it deserts us when we fail, whereas self-compassion can proudly step in at this point of failure and be there through the highs and the lows.

With self-compassion, we don't need perfection; we are kind towards ourselves, embracing ourselves as we are, warts and all. We are patient and gentle with ourselves, as we would be with another person. We can distinguish between making a mistake or a poor choice and being a failure as a person.

In Dr Neff's popular TEDx Talk, she discusses the three core components of self-compassion.

The first is fairly obvious: self-kindness, being kind to ourselves rather than judging ourselves harshly. Think of how you would respond to a friend who had fucked up versus how you would normally respond to yourself.

The second component she looks at is common humanity. The ways in which we're similar, rather than different. The fact that a defining characteristic of being human is to feel and to experience setbacks and to learn. Remember what Alexander Pope said: 'To err is human ...'? We all have that in common. The we're-all-in-this-together approach that relaxes the perfectionist side of things, enabling us to just be gorgeously imperfect humans.

The third component for Dr Neff is mindfulness, which we've already touched on in Chapter 2. Being non-judgmentally aware of how we are, as we are, in the moment that we're in. Accepting the fact that we're having a hard time enables compassion.

Her findings around the impact on our well-being of being a harsh self-critic versus being more self-compassionate resonated with me the most: we assume that being hard on ourselves will propel us further to achieve all that we want to achieve when, in reality, research shows that it does the opposite.

When we speak negatively to ourselves – and believe it – we launch an attack on ourselves. Our bodies produce cortisol – the stress hormone with which I am all too familiar – as a way to cope, which makes us feel anxious, which makes us feel fearful. Our body goes into protection and survival mode, which means the motivation we thought we were getting is pretty much out of reach. On the other hand, if we choose compassion and giving care to ourselves, our bodies get the signal to reduce the cortisol and, instead, produce oxytocin and opiates – two natural feel-good hormones. This makes us feel safe and comforted and better equipped to forge ahead.

For me, it was only when I really got in there and started to swap out my narrative and my self-talk, and accept that self-compassion wasn't just a nice idea but something that would impact me positively, on a biological level, that the anxiety in my body started to settle and I started to feel better.

It's a lot more than a kumbaya concept about being your own best friend. Self-compassion research is becoming more and more prevalent, and the evidence shows that it contributes hugely to strong mental health. Those with higher levels of self-compassion are said to experience less stress, less anxiety and less depression while also experiencing more happiness, more life satisfaction and better motivation, according to Queen Neff.

Consider these self-talk swaps that take you from self-critical to self-compassionate:

SELF-CRITICAL	SELF-COMPASSIONATE
I really fucked up, I'm an idiot.	I made a mistake, how can I remedy this?
I failed to get everything on my to-do list done, again.	I'm doing the best that I can, maybe I'm expecting too much of myself.
I'm feeling anxious again, clearly I am not coping.	My body is trying to tell me that something right now is too much for me, what might that be? How can I make myself feel a little bit better?
I didn't make it to the gym today, I need to go three times a week at least.	I listened to my body today; it told me that I needed a rest and that was a good use of my time, I'll go for a walk later.

So what can we do?

First of all, know that self-compassion is something that anyone can develop – it's a skill, not a personality trait – but this takes time and practice. Essentially, self-compassion is allowing yourself to give yourself what you need in the moment. It might just be a cup of tea. For a mother whose baby won't stop screaming, it might be two minutes to breathe or cry and tell herself that things will be OK.

We need to bring our awareness gently towards the fact that, no matter how things may seem on social media, everybody struggles to keep all of the plates spinning all of the time. It's OK to put a few of them down. Together, we can let ourselves off the hook.

Instead of thinking, *Oh, I should have done this* or *I should be doing more of this*, write down exactly what you would say to a friend who talked negatively about themselves. Even go so far as to write it as a letter to a friend but then read it as if it's for you.

How often have you told a friend, 'You have a lot on, you need some time for you'?

To bring self-compassion into your own life, ask yourself questions such as 'How can I help?' or 'What can I do to support you?' Notice when you go into harsh critic mode and say, 'OK, I'm turning down the volume on you now' or when you're haranguing yourself for not achieving everything on your to-do list, gently switch to a more compassionate alternative. Write it down if you have to and really do it; over time you'll start to believe it and you will positively impact the way you feel at a biological level.

Self-compassion.org has plenty of exercises and guided meditations to choose from and I recommend getting involved. Though, overall, I'm suggesting you cut things from your daily to-do list, a five-minute self-compassion exercise is a worthy addition. And keep bringing yourself back to do those essential components of self-compassion: self-kindness, common humanity and mindfulness.

For me, with self-compassion, the phrase 'you can do anything but you can't do everything' becomes softer than it sounded initially; it's like giving yourself permission to let some things go.

Sleep
Another essential addition and the priority to beat all other priorities has to be sleep.

Among its litany of benefits, which you'll find clearly laid out in the incredible book *Why We Sleep* by Matthew Walker, good-quality sleep makes it far easier to handle the unavoidable spinning plates of life; it makes us more resilient, more capable of moderating stress and anxiety, and it's one of the most powerful tools in your armoury to protect you against the plague of burnout.

Though we're now learning about its indisputable importance, for a very long time, sleep just wasn't popular. It wasn't respected - and, for that, we can blame science, as why we need it has only recently been explained to us. It got in the way of productivity, limiting our ability to perform around the clock, and in the eyes of big companies, sleep held them back from the profits they were after. 'I'll sleep when I'm dead' was a phrase you'd commonly hear from the mouths of hard-working go-getters who saw sleep as nothing more than an inconvenience. To get by on a few hours of shut-eye - or to pull an all-nighter at the office - was the reserve of those most motivated, those who really wanted to succeed in life.

If you were sleeping an eight-hour night in 1990s corporate America, could you really claim to be working hard enough? Would you really progress? Probably not. We looked at those for whom sleep was at the bottom of their priority list and thought, *Wow, that's impressive.* Why sleep when you can caffeinate?

I have certainly felt bad about myself for the fact that I couldn't seem to sacrifice sleep for productivity, not that I've ever worked in a company where I've been expected to stay in the office all night. Was sleep just for the weak?

Inevitably, this very unhealthy (and quite frankly fucking stupid) perception of sleep caught up with these types. They burned out. They got sick. They got depressed. They needed medication to sleep and medication to stay awake. Their relationships suffered. Their ability to perform at work suffered.

Then, the companies started to notice it too.

Sure, overworked and overtired employees might yield results in the short-term, but if you're hoping to continue in business for more than a few years, this was a pressure cooker waiting to blow. Eloquently put by Matthew Walker, 'The elastic band of sleep deprivation can stretch only so far before it snaps.' Productivity went down. Profits went down. Employees, no longer able to cope, wound up quitting. Companies lost their best assets. Suddenly nobody was benefitting from this idea of getting by on less sleep and hacking your way through with gallons of coffee.

I write this as though I'm talking about the days of yore when, in reality, it's an issue that still has a long way to go in terms of the working world. We might physically leave the office at a reasonable time, but, to go back to Arianna Huffington as a perfect example, she was still sitting up in bed at midnight pinging emails back and forth. Her phone was still the first thing she picked up in the morning, engaging with work-related queries before she'd even brushed her teeth. She was working around the clock – literally – and for too many people this is still their reality.

Changing our attitudes towards sleep is something that needs to be done at an individual level but also on a wider societal level. With more and more research emerging over the past two decades, we're starting to see sleep for the tool it really is. We're seeing it as perhaps the most productive activity of all. Some of the more progressive companies and business people out there are certainly beginning to acknowledge that sleep is not just something we have to do each night, but something that is intrinsically linked to the success we're all after.

This approach helps companies to view sleep as essential for profit, and, at the end of the day, that's what they're all about.

But for us mere mortals, sleep isn't just about professional success. It's essential for every biochemical reaction in our bodies. Every component of well-being depends on it. It is one of the most important things we can do in order to stay healthy, both physically and mentally. If sleep were really unnecessary, as some perceive it to be, you can guarantee it would have been weeded out by evolution over time. But Mother Nature wants us to sleep for a reason. It's a vital function necessary for our survival. And if you don't respect that, she will sure as hell let you know she's not happy.

Today, I am incredibly proud of my ability to sleep, the quality of sleep I get, and the routine I have installed around it, which involves everything you've already heard of such as removing tech from the room, avoiding caffeine, keeping the room temperature cool, reading before bed, etc. The fact that I ensure I get my eight hours a night is now my badge of honour rather than the other way around. (Newborn-related sleep deprivation aside, of course.)

I could write a chapter dedicated entirely to sleep, but time (and my word count) is of the essence and Matthew Walker's book, which aims to revise our cultural appreciation of sleep and reverse our neglect of it with scientific accuracy, already has it covered in ways I'd never be able to. Do make a note to read his book if you haven't yet, but, for now, I'll point out some of Walker's interesting sleep facts, which I hope will help you to think a little differently about your next slumber session.

According to Walker, scientist and Professor of Neuroscience and Psychology at Berkeley in California, 99 per cent of humans need eight hours of sleep to function optimally. Less than 1 per cent of the population can claim to 'get by' on less than six hours of sleep per night. The rest of us will experience impairment of function, end of.

Nothing good comes from a lack of sleep. Aside from the physical health risks, such as risk of inflammation, compromised immunity, heart disease, cancer and more, sleep disruption lowers your productivity regardless of whether you believe it or not. Walker says that when we are sleep deprived we are fooled into believing we are coping better than we are. A lack of sleep impairs your ability to make rational decisions and to control your emotions. Proper sleep calibrates our emotional brain circuits.

Sleep disruption contributes to all major psychiatric conditions, including depression and anxiety. Having ten nights of six-hour sleeps is equal in damage to one all-nighter, as is six nights of four-hour sleeps.

There isn't an organ in the human body that isn't detrimentally impaired when we don't get enough sleep. Sleep maintains your gut microbiome which we now know correlates strongly with mental and physical well-being. Sleep, Matthew Walker would even suggest, is the preeminent force in the healthy trinity, among which a balanced diet and exercise are included. It is the single most effective thing we can do to reset our brain and body health each day. For this and countless other reasons, sleep is one priority you cannot cut. In fact, you should only add to it, revelling in this delightful biological drive, complete with indulgent pyjamas and luxurious bed sheets, without feeling one bit guilty about it.

Essentialism

On a more practical level, when you've made a start on implementing self-compassion into your day – and sleeping better too – you need to look at the rest of your 'priorities' and trim the fat.

Sticking with the same number of to-dos on your list and adding compassion and the odd nap in for good measure won't be enough; you need to seriously re-evaluate what's important to you and what is not. Even at that, something might be important to you, but it might not be feasible for you to include it. For example, you might really want to attend a one-hour yoga class every morning, but if this isn't doable for you – maybe you have kids who need to be taken to school at that time – that's OK.

Write down what you are expecting of yourself on a daily basis. Circle the actual priorities. Then, without feeling ashamed or defeated, be honest with yourself about what you can feasibly achieve within your own personal bandwidth. It's not about giving up and it's not about settling, it's about doing what you can and want to do without compromising on the quality of your time, your well-being and your work. How much of what you're doing is because you think you should be doing it rather than because you want to be doing it? For example, do I really want to play tag rugby? Sure, I'd like the social interaction and sometimes I feel guilty knowing that my husband would like me to join him but, nah, I'm actually not excited by sports and I don't need one more thing to do that pleases someone other than myself. I'd much rather stay at home and have a bath, and that is something I now schedule time for.

I've been hugely influenced by 'Essentialism', a lifestyle manifesto put forward by author Greg McKeown. He defines his idea very simply as 'less but better'. Though he applies it mostly to a professional environment – where we deal with countless interruptions and distractions throughout the day – for me, it easily crosses over into private life too.

In his bestselling book, *Essentialism: The Disciplined Pursuit of Less*, McKeown encourages us to separate the 'vital few from the trivial many' and live our lives by design (something we've decided on) rather than by default (the swirling black hole of to-dos we get lost in every day). Thereby articulating in just one sentence what I've attempted to say in a whole chapter. McKeown writes: 'Only once you give yourself the permission to stop trying to do it all, to stop saying yes to everyone, can you make your highest contribution towards the things that really matter.' At work, he says we should ask ourselves, 'What is essential?', and eliminate the rest.

In life, I suggest that on top of what is absolutely essential, you consider what makes you feel good, which might include time for nothing more than unencumbered thought; then you'll know what edits to make.

Apart from the fact that your own well-being will suffer if you take on everything at once, you also have to consider the fact that our brains just can't apply an adequate level of focus to that many things in one day. This is especially relevant when it comes to your professional work. Yes, you can do anything, and you can probably do it all, but according to the science, you can't do everything well. You can do some things really well, and if you weigh yourself down with an endless list of to-dos, while you'll probably be able to squeeze it all in, the value and the focus just won't be there. Turns out, we're great multi-taskers, but multi-focusing is not our forte.

For a long time, at least professionally, I tried to take on a lot of things at once - and, being self-employed, that might be twenty different professional projects percolating through my mind in the space of an hour. I have always prided myself on the fact that I have my finger in so many pies but, recently, I've had to assess whether it's really working for me. Every now and then, I'll observe that while I feel incredibly busy, I'm not getting a whole lot done. As McKeown would say, I'm making one millimetre of success in one million directions or I'm majoring in minor activities.

The thing is, when you work for yourself, the word no becomes even harder to say than normal because everything feels like an opportunity. If you say no one too many times, suddenly you find yourself in I'm-basically-unemployed territory, which is scary as hell for those of us doing it alone. 'She said no before so we won't ask her again.' So, you say yes as a way to future-proof yourself.

You feel lucky and grateful for every potential lead and so you cast your net far and wide in the hope of catching at least one lucrative fish. But while I can technically switch up what I'm working on every half hour – there is more than enough time in the day for it – I've noticed that the quality of what I produce and the quality of my concentration goes drastically downhill. It takes me far longer to finish a project in its entirety when I veer away from essentialism. I'm also more stressed out and frazzled from the flip-flopping of it all and more frustrated by the fact that I don't seem to be getting anywhere.

And it's not just because I'm picking up my phone a little too regularly to binge on infomania, which is definitely a huge part of it. I splinter my focus across a series of tasks to such an extent that I'm doing lots of things, but I'm not doing any of them particularly well.

Sophie Leroy, Associate Professor at the University of Washington Bothell School of Business, called this 'attention residue' in her 2009 paper entitled 'Why is it so hard to do my work?'. Through various experiments, she observed the following phenomenon:

when you flit from one cognitive task to another, your concentration basically goes to shit. She worded it more nicely than that, of course. Even though you might think you are now giving all of your focus to the task at hand, a residual portion of your attention remains on the task that preceded it, using up your cognitive batteries, and your performance on the current task suffers. This happens easily as we flit from emails to meetings to Instagram to to-do lists and then when it's time to really focus on something more cognitively demanding, we feel as though our heads are packed with the endless open tabs of a cluttered web browser. Keep doing that throughout the day, every day, which most of us do, and we find ourselves 'functioning with a reduced cognitive capacity'. It's for this reason that I have found myself spending an hour on a task that could have taken me twenty minutes or why writing this book has been so challenging and why my phone is currently locked away in a drawer.

Infomania sounds like something out of an George Orwell novel but, in today's digital world, it's par for the course. Infomania refers to the compulsive desire to check up on and accumulate news and information, typically via our mobile phones. With infomania you become overloaded with information that builds up in your brain – there's too much to process at any one time and it becomes even more overwhelming when you add in constant interruptions from various notifications, calls, emails and texts.

A 2005 study by Glenn Wilson showed that infomania can affect our ability to problem-solve. In fact, he found that it can be just as debilitating and harmful to our cognition as losing a whole night's sleep. I believe this information binge has a few other unwanted side-effects: it increases anxiety, it skews our focus and concentration, and, in some instances, it can desensitise us to such an extent that we're no longer clear on what's important to us and what's not.

Again, it comes back to deciding on your priorities – doing less but better – and then taking one thing at a time, and trying your best to finish one task before you crack on to the next, so that when you do, your mind is right there with you. In order to get this book done, while maintaining the more immediate work I had going on, I had to get disciplined with my time. For starters, I set up time limits on my social media apps on my phone. Like an automatic tic, I would reach for my phone after writing just a few lines as a kind of reward. As this was so ingrained in my behaviour, I had to get tough by putting this measure in place.

At first I would continue to pick up my phone only to be reminded that I couldn't get into the apps (I would only allow myself thirty minutes a day, which is more than enough) but, after a while, my automatic brain caught up with this new habit and the addict-like need to go for it began to wane. I also noticed that Fridays were always quieter on email, so I dedicated this day every week to working on the book; my dog would go to day care so I wouldn't have to keep him entertained (he's young and demanding), and the rest of my tasks for the week were already taken care of in the previous days, so on Fridays I had very few distractions. Then Saturday and Sunday would come, where I would shut off my work brain entirely, giving me the space to restore my cognitive bandwidth.

 PAUSE FOR THOUGHT

Sure, you've heard the phrase, 'You can do anything but you can't do everything' a million times before. Have you ever given it a chance to sink in and consider what this means in the context of your own life?

Though other schools of thought will tell you that you can have it all and that you should go for it all – think of all the things you could do! – let me remind you that you are only one person. And there are only twenty-four hours in a day, eight of which you now know you should spend asleep.

You're super and you're a woman (or a man), but you don't have to be superwoman (or, yes, superman). Not all of the time. You don't have to keep pushing forward. You don't have to be constantly juggling. You can allow yourself, with confidence and compassion, to put something down on the table. You can choose to say no to the stuff that's not really important.

You can respect that you're working with a particular cognitive bandwidth that starts to deplete from the moment you get up, so that you should only use it on the stuff that matters. You can slow things down. You can do less, knowing it will be less but better. Instead of forging your way upstream and battling a raging torrent, you can allow yourself to float along the bayou (and, yes, I did have to Google the accurate descriptions of various bodies of water) for a while.

If you have far too much going on, something's gotta give. Don't let the thing that gives be you or your sleep. If you're going to lean in, do so with compassion and awareness; don't lean in so far that you fall flat on your face.

CHAPTER 4

Truth #4
Where there is failure, there is always opportunity

FAILING SUCKS. It's not something anybody wants to experience at any point in their lifetime, let alone embrace. It's shitty, it's sour and it's uncomfortable, and you're well within your rights to wallow into a tub of Ben & Jerry's for a few hours when, try as you might, things just go tits up.

Our desire to avoid failure is often the reason why we gravitate towards books like this one in the first place: we want to be as well equipped as possible in order to keep ourselves well away from failure.

For so long, it seemed to me that the goal wasn't to become resilient to failure or to learn better how to cope with it, but to not have to deal with it at all. Until recently, I would have done anything to avoid a failure of any kind, such was my disdain for the feelings it brought on. It's fair to say that most of us are brought up in a context where failure is bad news. Failure usually went hand in hand with a punishment of some kind. Failure meant we were cut off from opportunities. Failure might have meant disappointing someone, and we don't much like that either. More often than not, failure would put our self-worth in jeopardy.

But it's not just that we've been nurtured in this way, it's in our nature too. We've evolved biologically to fear failure because, at one point, failure wasn't just a rap on the knuckles or the feeling of shame for not having done a good enough job, it meant death, literally! Failure to hunt food? Failure to win a fight with a predator? No marks for effort back then.

Today, we operate in much the same way. We apply the same amount of fear to the idea of failure as we did when our survival was in question, despite the fact that the stakes today are significantly lower. In fact, you might even say that our aversion towards it has increased, possibly because these days our failures are more public than ever, thanks to social media, and our successes are so strongly linked with our self-worth. But because we're human and despite all we've done to avoid it, failure still finds a way to bite us in the ass. And when it does, it knocks us for six. We perceive it as confirmation of our inadequacy, confirmation of our subpar self-worth and confirmation that we shouldn't try again – maybe that we shouldn't try at all. It beats the crap out of us and all that we learn is what we already know: failure sucks.

But here's a thought: for so long, we've failed to understand failure. Contrary to how it feels when we experience it, I believe that failing is not just inevitable but an incredibly necessary and highly valuable, if not particularly nice, part of life. Like your very own Batman, it serves as your life's anti-hero. You mightn't want it but you need it and here are just some of the reasons why:

o It sharpens your instincts. Like a compass, it helps you to course-correct, albeit quite severely, in the direction of your life's path and your true purpose.
o It smacks you in the face with a reminder of what's really important and what's not.
o It brings your core values into focus.
o It lets you know where your limits are, what you can handle, what you're capable of and what's too much.
o It provides a contrast so that we can know and appreciate when things go right. Without negative we don't really know what positive is. Failure is a useful negative; it makes the good stuff in life much sweeter.
o It provides the plot twists in your life story, without which you'd be bored senseless.
o It enables vulnerability, something that, as I suggest later on, is an unskippable ingredient for happiness.

Without failure, we cannot know that we are resilient. We certainly can't increase our resilience without it. What's more, it's only by coming face to face with failure that can we develop our resilience. Think about it: your resilience can only be tested and strengthened in the face of adversity. If everything works out for you all of the time, you have no way to gauge your resilience. If nothing ever goes wrong for you, you're probably nowhere near as resilient as you would be if you had tripped up from time to time.

Avoiding failure is not something to strive for but increasing your resilience is. And the only way to increase your resilience? Fail. Ultimately, without failing or stumbling to some degree, our personal growth suffers.

A note on resilience

When we think about something or someone as having a resilient nature, we think of it or them as being resistant to breaking. That's not what resilience is about. It's not about being unbreakable – that is not the goal. Instead, resilience is the capacity we have to bounce back from or adjust to difficulties. It's less rigid and more about developing our emotional elasticity or flexibility. Your resilience is a measure of how quickly and how easily you can go back to your relative state of normality after having that normality put under strain. Resilient people aren't impervious to strain; they feel it and then bounce back.

For me though, we can go one step further with failure, and this is the crux of this chapter.

Where there is failure, there isn't just learning or personal growth, there's opportunity too. This is true, provided you're willing to reframe it in this way.

Similar in ways to stress, failing is not harmful – just as stress is not harmful – when we choose to react to it appropriately. It's not so much the presence of failure or stress in our bodies that's the problem – we can't really avoid either of these things if we're really living a full life anyway – the problem lies within our response to them.

In a 2009 study reported in *Scientific American*, something known colloquially as 'the loser effect' was noted. Its antithesis, 'the winner effect', is something we can all relate to. When we (humans or animals) win at something, our brain releases a surge of the neurotransmitters dopamine and testosterone. When we are successful at something, these chemicals serve to rewire our brains, telling our brain cells to keep doing whatever it was they were doing that led to our success in the first place.

Think of when you find yourself on a winning streak and everything seems to be working out for you. The loser effect works in the opposite way and is best understood by the old adage of 'when it rains it pours'.

When monkeys in this particular study made a mistake in a trial, they went on to perform far worse than the monkeys who had made no mistakes at all. Their failure and reaction to it impeded their ability to concentrate later on. 'In other words, they were thrown off by their mistakes rather than learning from them,' explained *Scientific American*.

In a 2010 study quoted on sciencedirect.com, a group of people who had been dieting were given pizza. They were convinced that this had ruined their diet and, after eating the pizza, this group were reported to have eaten 50 per cent more cookies than those who were not on a diet at all – one slip-up was perceived as a reason to just give up entirely. This tells me that we don't naturally respond to failure by learning from our mistakes. We naturally respond by getting stuck in a cycle that perpetuates further failure. As such, we have to make a point of consciously stepping away from this and reframing our failure by looking for the silver lining – and keeping our eyes peeled for the opportunity – if we're going to move beyond it.

When I view failure as an opportunity, it removes my fear of it. It makes me less concerned with avoiding it. In fact, it becomes something you would go so far as to invite into your life; it's the cauliflower that you loathe entirely, but that you know will be good for you in the long run. (Clearly I have no fond feelings for this poor vegetable; if I have caused offence to those of you who chow down on cauliflower mashed potato, cauliflower pizza bases, cauliflower rice or just plain old chunks of cauliflower as it is, I do apologise.)

If something you're trying works out, great, but if it doesn't, you're afforded a fresh start and a blank slate. You're afforded insight into what didn't work and what could be done differently. And you get to try again from this arguably more advantageous position. When you fail and try again and it goes your way, I can guarantee that your second shot will always be better than whatever you could have achieved the first time around.

Someone for whom failure was the ultimate life opportunity was a man called Noah McVicker. In the 1930s, he invented a pliable, putty-like substance that was intended to clean coal off dirty walls, rejuvenating the wallpaper without having to redo the whole thing. It worked well and served its purpose for a time, but with the shift away from coal fires (electric and gas heating became more popular, while someone else invented washable vinyl wallpaper), his product was no longer needed. The sales dried up and put him out of business. In this more traditional sense where success is linked with how well a product is selling, McVicker had what he considered an epic failure on his hands.

He hired his nephew, Joe McVicker, who wanted to help save the company from bankruptcy. There had been a lot of product lying around Noah and Joe's houses and one day, Joe's sister-in-law, who was a primary school teacher, made note of the fact that her kids seemed to really like playing with this putty stuff. It was easier for them than playing with traditional clay, and a lot less messy too. She joked with Joe about how it could be remarketed as a play-thing for kids. He figured he had nothing to lose, the company had already failed, so why not give it a shot? And that's how the incredibly successful Play-Doh brand came to be: a fun, non-toxic toy with which I'm sure every person who reads this book will be familiar. (I can still recall its sugary smell.)

For the McVickers, it was a totally unintended success afforded by the opportunity of failure. It didn't just fall into their laps though, it required them to really think about the potential for opportunity in what was no longer working and, of course, it required that they try again. Their story is one of my favourites in that it demonstrates to the rest of the world that we might only be one small adjustment away from turning a failure on its head and making it infinitely better than it ever was before. That maybe it's worth getting to that point of failure in order to clear your path and find the real opportunity.

As a perfectionist, though, with an ego that bruises like a peach, I must admit that I've never enjoyed failure. I get very upset by it. I wouldn't say I handle it all that well in the moment, but after I've allowed myself to indulge in the emotions that come with it - something that I think is very important; it's never a good idea to ignore and bury how you feel and it's all part of the process - I will experience a clarity like nothing else.

I will wake up the lines of communication between the me that does and says things and the me that knows things: my intuition. We'll be exploring how to tap into your intuition more in Chapter 9, but if there's one quickfire way to switch it on, allow yourself the opportunity to fail.

In 2019, my first book was published in America. When I heard about the US book deal, I figured I'd made it, only to discover how incredibly hard it is to get a look-in in such an enormous and hugely competitive market. A few months after they'd been published, I remember asking my publishers how many books I'd sold and nearly falling off the chair when they told me that a sum total of 110 copies had been sold across all of the US. Embarrassingly, I had bought about twelve of those myself and gifted them to those I had met when in New York promoting the book. I could not believe the numbers and I felt so foolish for thinking I could be successful there.

Shortly after this, I was writing a beauty column, which I adored, for a national newspaper each week but with budget cuts it was contributors like me who were first sent to the gallows. Fine, no big deal, this is why, as a freelancer, you have several things going on at any one time, so that you're never stuck.

But then my other old reliables started to evaporate too. I had a great relationship with an editor for another magazine, and was writing lots of regular features for her. It was becoming my main source of income and I was so glad of it. But then she left her job to go somewhere new and the new editor wanted to change things up and make her own mark, so that work instantly dried up. The same thing happened with about four or five other gigs I had going.

What's more, between the drying up of my regular work and the amount of time I had spent plugging the US, I realised that I hadn't earned any income in months. I was spending my tax money (don't worry, I eventually paid it back) and though I appeared successful as a 'published author', the reality didn't quite measure up.

When my husband asked me if I was going to be able to top up our joint account in order to help pay the mortgage that month, I had to say, 'Eh, no actually.'

'Have you any money coming in?' he asked.

Now it's not possible to know in advance how you'll sustain your income when you're a freelancer (and, as a result, it's not a great way to live if you're anxious like me) but I couldn't think of any opportunities coming my way that would translate into cold, hard cash. And so naturally I thought to myself, *Could it be that you're failing? This just might not be happening for you. It might be time to give up.*

I told my mom all of the above, expecting her to say something along the lines of 'you've got to keep going', but she echoed my thoughts exactly, saying, 'It might be worth considering going back to a full-time job where you can depend on a salary.'

And so I slipped under the parapet, feeling sorry for myself, feeling defeated, feeling bruised – and I wallowed there for about a week.

Then, when I had got used to the idea that things weren't working out and the thought no longer made me want to blubber into a cup of tea as I distracted myself with reruns of *Friends*, I decided to look for the opportunity. I first had to show myself some self-compassion in that a lot of those lost gigs were completely out of my control and not my fault; it was no reflection on me (well, I certainly hope not). America? Well, that was a necessary dose of reality: if it was easy, everyone would do it. And this is why most people don't try. I told myself that I was lucky enough to have had the opportunity and it's not a failure if it isn't over, so give it time. Be patient and keep trying.

I then, finally, reached the point of clarity that I needed in order to bounce back: I realised I was focusing so much of my time and energy on what I could not control. I was relying on sources of income that were incredibly precarious. If I continued this way, I'd wind up feeling like a failure again and again. I realised that in having all of these work commitments evaporate, I had nothing but time. I viewed it as a golden opportunity to put it to use.

If I wasn't earning any money, I might as well get busy doing something that at least I could control. I decided that in order to sustain my lifestyle – I did not want to go back to a full-time job unless it was absolutely necessary – I was going to need to rely upon myself and create my own opportunities rather than wait for someone else to send one my way. I knew that anything worth doing would take time, and even more time before it would generate any kind of income, and that the likelihood of failure was high, but I had nothing really to lose from where I was at. I could give something a go. If nothing changed within a year, I could go back to the drawing board.

So, I started working on my own anxiety podcast, the podcast version of my first book, *Owning It*. It was a lot of work getting from zero listeners right up to 50,000 people tuning in on a weekly basis. Sometimes I figured it wasn't worth doing, but after almost a year I had built up enough of an audience to generate some money each month through advertising. It wasn't much, but it was me who had created the opportunity for myself. It also resulted in a spike in book sales around the world because of listeners finding the podcast who had never heard of the book. My previous book sales in America weren't a reflection on me, it was that nobody knew the book existed, but now I had the chance to change that.

It also led to further opportunities to come and speak with groups of staff at various companies because so many of them had been listening and reading. Ultimately, the opportunity I had made gave me a platform that I could continue to build upon, whereas had I continued writing those pieces, which I thought at the time were so crucial to my success, I may not have tasted the sourness of failure, but I would also not have grown and had the clarity to create the career and the lifestyle I wanted in the first place.

I'm still creating it every day, but had everything worked out as I had hoped when I first went freelance, I wouldn't be doing what I'm doing now.

Now, of course, it doesn't escape me that I was in a very fortunate position to be able to keep trying and have the financial support of my husband – I know not everyone has that luxury – but this is something I could still have endeavoured to do while working a full-time job, which is what I did when I first went out on my own. It's not easy, it requires a hustle that needs regular replenishment and a willingness to think of failure in a new way.

I approach failure in a very specific way. First, I surrender to the feeling that failure brings with it. I understand that I'm wired not to like it. Then I choose to override that wiring and reframe it as an opportunity.

Note that, in doing this, when you reframe failure as a chance for opportunity, it doesn't mean you're thrilled that it's happening. It doesn't mean you don't throw your toys out of the pram. It doesn't mean that it won't feel like shit. It doesn't mean you enjoy failure. So, don't put yourself under pressure to not feel bad when you experience a setback. Feel it.

In the tug of war between how you feel - your mind is threatened by the presence of failure - and how you think you should feel, drop the rope. Don't force yourself to summon your inner Dalai Lama and not to react to it. To do this if you're feeling really crap about something would be an act of inauthenticity.

If you try to find opportunity in failure on the very day that the shit hits the fan, whether it's a job you learn that you didn't get or you've come to the conclusion that a relationship is no longer working, it will not work. This is not the time to try to look for silver linings. In fact, I really hate it when I'm in the wallowing phase and someone suggests that it might all have happened for a reason. As though you should just jump straight to the positives there and then. As though feeling negative is really bad for you and something to push under the rug. Don't be the person that says this to someone who's just experienced a failure (or something not working out) and if someone says it to you just ignore it. Until the dust has settled for you, this is anything but helpful and a useless exercise.

I find it far better to say to someone in this moment something like, 'Yeah, I know it sucks, I'm really sorry.' Sometimes, you just want someone to say it's OK to feel how you're feeling. You don't need to be told when your heart has just shattered into a million tiny pieces that time heals all wounds. You're not ready for that yet. The timing around how you reframe your perceived failure is key. Being upset is OK and very necessary in order to clear the cobwebs. Letting yourself cry flushes the cortisol out of your system and is incredibly therapeutic. When I feel a cry coming on, I welcome it. Crying is like polishing up an old vintage piece of furniture. It doesn't look too pretty until you've given it a good scrub, after which you realise maybe it's not all that bad.

When that initial and perfectly natural disappointment has settled back to some level of normality again, which it absolutely will, that's precisely the time to swoop in and turn things around. You can ask yourself questions such as:

o 'How would I approach this again?'
o 'What would I do differently?'
o 'What worked and what didn't work?'
o 'Do I really care about this thing that I'm doing?'

- 'Do I really want it?'
- 'Is there an opportunity here somewhere?'

It might not always be an opportunity to the level that the McVickers enjoyed (I only wish I could tell you that every failure will make you a multimillionaire), but anything that gives you awareness and growth is always an opportunity in my book (literally).

By approaching failure in this way, you're not trying to change how you react; if you care about something you are going to react, and whatever you're feeling it's valid and worth honouring. You allow for all of that because sometimes accepting your mind and emotions as they are is the most useful strategy you can have. Then, when the time is right, you make it work for you. I consider it the 'bend and snap' of failure, a foolproof technique borrowed and reimagined through a psychological lens from *Legally Blonde*'s Elle Woods. Bend into the feeling, surrender to it, then snap it to suit you. The bend and snap of failure. (I'll get my coat.)

 PAUSE FOR THOUGHT

Think back to a recent failure you've experienced, or a perceived failure. What came of it? Were there any hidden opportunities? Did failing on one path lead you to another path? Did a breakup open you up to the possi-

bility of meeting someone new, someone with whom you're far better suited?

How did the failure impact your resilience? Did you find that, after a period of time, that Friedrich Nietzsche – and later Kelly Clarkson – was right when he said, 'What doesn't kill you makes you stronger'?

Did your elastic band get even better at bouncing back? It's true that failure sucks. But it's also true that failure is an opportunity in disguise if you are courageous enough to look.

Truth #5
A willingness to be vulnerable makes you invulnerable: understanding the vulnerability paradox

FINALLY, A CHAPTER dedicated entirely to the theme you'll find woven throughout the whole of *Naked* - vulnerability.

So, what exactly is vulnerability?

It's a word we're hearing a *lot* these days. Along with anxiety, vulnerability is a common feature of the millennial lexicon, but there is a slight difference between how vulnerability is traditionally defined or perceived - as something negative to be avoided – and how I choose to view it – as something positive to be embraced.

Defined in the dictionary as 'the quality or state of being exposed to the possibility of being attacked or harmed, either physically or emotionally', it's understandable that few of us would really relish that feeling, let alone want to own it. Nobody wants to be vulnerable in any aspect of their life, but the reality is that not a single person walking on earth has managed to escape it. We're born vulnerable and we die vulnerable.

Whether it's emotional – such as having feelings for someone and hoping they will be reciprocated – or physical – death will catch up with all of us eventually (sorry) – it's a sure thing; a central tenet of the human experience. And if there's anyone you look at and think, *Wow, they're just not vulnerable in any way, they are made of steel*, you're wrong. Either they are feeling it but doing their best to hide it or they've got a head start on this chapter and they've learned to be comfortable with their vulnerability. It's one or the other, of that you can be certain.

Vulnerability can be experienced in every conceivable aspect of life. You can feel it anytime you're not sure of what you're doing or any time you're not firing on all cylinders. You can feel vulnerable when you're under the weather or in a relationship when you share something personal about yourself and worry about how the other person will react. You can feel vulnerable at work when you're asked to give a presentation and all eyes are on you. You can feel vulnerable when you take your new baby home from hospital and don't have the first clue how to look after it. Though we might not recognise it as such, the vulnerability we feel here does stem from a fear of being attacked or judged, and given that our brain's primary concern has and always will be our safety and survival, it makes sense that we want to avoid anything that puts is in a vulnerable position.

Again, vulnerability today is a lot easier to handle than it was when our brains were developing. If we were sick back then or if we were asleep when a predator was around or we were rejected by our tribe as a result of misbehaving, it would be likely that death was on the cards. Today, our survival is probably not in question when we go to give a presentation at work or when we open ourselves up to a new romance after having been hurt before, but we still hold the same aversion towards anything that feels as though we are in harm's way. It might not be physical harm but it can certainly feel as though we're at risk of emotional harm.

I don't need scientific research to convince you of the presence of vulnerability. We can all recall a time when we've felt vulnerable in some way (for me, it's something I feel every day). Yet for too long, we've been trying to exist as though we're not vulnerable, which, as a result (certainly in my own experience), creates huge amounts of tension within us, leading to pressure, stress, anxiety, issues at work and in personal relationships, and much more. We dodge vulnerability like the plague – in much the same way we dodge failure.

And even though our vulnerability is inherent, we try to go about our days, we try to present ourselves to the world as though we're not vulnerable at all. Without being fully aware of it, we are constantly resisting how things are, and while that's something we might be good at doing for a while, eventually the cracks will start to appear. For me, the crack was crippling anxiety. I wasn't feeling well, I was in a new job and, on the inside, I felt strongly that I couldn't handle it while, on the outside, I tried desperately to portray that I could. My unwillingness to admit my vulnerability led to a very unavoidable vulnerability manifesting itself in my everyday experience: panic attacks.

Unfortunately, though, we've been culturally conditioned – and biologically, thanks to our need to survive – to never show it.

In a more modern scenario, consider the phrase that I heard a lot growing up: 'Never air your dirty laundry in public.' This was widely accepted as a rule, certainly for my parents' generation and their parents before them. Don't ever show a vulnerability in your marriage to the outside world, for example. Definitely keep quiet about a mental health issue in your family. In fact, somewhere down the not so distant line of a friend's family tree there was a male relative who struggled with his mental health and, as was the remedy for the time, was sent to an asylum. Rather than ever have anybody find about this family 'shame', they decided instead to tell everyone he had died. Imagine! It was easier and more comfortable to fake a death than to reveal a vulnerability in the family.

Thankfully, we've come a long way since then but this reticence still exists. I remember when I first took to social media to open up about my anxiety. Texts flooded in from friends: 'Are you sure you want to put that out there?' This was in the very early days of mental health awareness on social media and was something of a foreign concept in a world that only showed the best bits.

Something you'll still hear today when training for a public-speaking engagement, for example, is: 'Don't let them see your fear.' Fearlessness is still the be all and end all. In many a workplace, the anti-vulnerability messaging has been along the lines of 'Fake it till you make it', and so on.

I remember trying to force Kelly Cutrone's book *If You Have to Cry, Go Outside* into my consciousness as I felt this idea of toughening up was key to success. I tried and tried but it just did not work for me; it required a resistance to my nature that felt counterproductive and anxiety-inducing. I really believed, at the time, that steeling myself was necessary to not just survive in the workplace but move forward. I looked at those who were at the top of their game, such as Ms Cutrone, and they seemed to possess pit bull levels of ferocity, while saying, 'Well you'd have to be like that to get to that level, wouldn't you?' There was no room for vulnerability in the professional sphere, they were never to overlap. With this understanding, I assumed that I wasn't going to get very far if I didn't seem like I could handle all of the things or if I had any weaknesses. I was much too soft. Showing my own Achilles' heels, of which there were many, would, I thought, only reflect badly on me and would only have a negative effect on my career.

But I was wrong. Eventually I realised another truth: a willingness to be vulnerable makes you invulnerable.

What?

Hear me out.

I really believe that by allowing ourselves to be vulnerable in our day-to-day lives, in our relationships and even our professional endeavours, we actually wind up achieving the strength and resilience we assumed that our vulnerability would take from us. By owning our vulnerability, we succeed in dismantling and subverting its original meaning. In doing this, we are no longer open to attack, we become invulnerable.

For this truth, I'm going so far as to introduce you to what I've found to be quite the game-changer: I call it the Vulnerability Paradox and it is as follows.

One well-known example is the character of Fat Amy, played by Rebel Wilson, in the *Pitch Perfect* movies. (Well, I mean 'well known' if you're a fan of musical comedies, of course.) Though she's very happy and confident in herself, she knows the world will perceive her weight as a vulnerability – it's something that not-so-nice people would use against her. And so rather than wait for the inevitable meanness she suspects will come her way, she takes her vulnerability and makes it hers. She owns it. She introduces herself as 'Fat Amy' before anybody else has the chance to comment on or point out her weight. Not in a 'poor me' way but in a 'this is who I am and I'm good with that' way. She reframes her vulnerability as armour and it works wonderfully. She projects her vulnerability back out to the world as a strength, and as a result she becomes invulnerable. Nobody can touch her.

If you've read my previous books or followed my rambling, mile-a-minute stories on Instagram, you will know that I am all for owning your vulnerability. I bang on about its importance daily, so much so my friends think I'm sponsored by vulnerability.

Inspired first and foremost by Brené Brown - if you aren't familiar with her work, I'm going to stop you right there and encourage you to dive into her TED Talks, her books, Netflix show, articles, the list goes on, and then come back to me - my life changed for the better (*hugely*) when I turned my attention to vulnerability. When I stopped denying my vulnerability and was willing to accept it as not just a part of my life to put up with but something to actually embrace, I started to feel more resilient than I ever had before. It has been the single most important step in getting on top of the anxiety that plagued me for so long.

It took a long time before I saw vulnerability as something acceptable, however, and even longer before I saw it as something to embrace and celebrate. For me, though, accepting it wasn't so much a choice I made one day, as something I did out of desperation. It was my last-ditch attempt at a coping mechanism that, as it turned out, would have saved me from a lot of suffering in the first place if I had only tapped into it sooner.

I remember trying to articulate how anxious I was to a former boss (the anxiety wasn't brought about by this specific job but I was struggling to hide it and somewhere, deep down, I figured it might be easier to address it), and I was riddled with worry that she would perceive me as not up to the task. Or unreliable.

It was actually during my interview for the role that I brought it up, which would have been considered the ultimate interview faux pas at the time. Interviews are a time to show only your best bits and give the best impression! Kelly Cutrone would probably have slammed the door in my face and told me to come back when I was made of stronger stuff.

This was the first job I'd gone for after having been out of work for several months in order to get better. I was not comfortable sharing my vulnerability whatsoever but, as I said, I felt I had no choice. I felt that, on some level, it would somehow protect me against disappointing them. I felt it was only fair to let this new company know what a bag of anxious (yet still capable!) bones they were about to employ. I figured that if I pretended as though I was totally fine, I would go home and instantly have a panic attack, worrying that sooner or later my anxiety would show and I'd let myself and everyone else down. However, in showing my vulnerability, she showed me hers. In the interview, she simply said she could totally empathise and that she was really sorry to hear that I'd had a hard time. She knew well what anxiety felt like and reassured me that I was not alone in it. 'We're all in it together,' she said, 'and we have to make work a place that helps our anxiety rather than adds to it.'

What she said was enough of a hint at her humaneness. Her story soon followed, though and, over coffee, I learned that she too found it all a bit tough sometimes. This was a new role for her too and she was feeling a little out of her depth. Learning this didn't make me think any less of her, it made me respect her more.

Her willingness to accept and normalise my vulnerability meant everything to me. I wasn't weak. I wasn't a bad hire. I was human and so was she. We gave ourselves permission to be authentic and I soon realised that I wasn't the only person who was vulnerable; we all are, yet we're all trying to pretend as though we're not.

My sharing of my vulnerability didn't have any negative impact on my job or how I was perceived – though I do acknowledge that I was lucky; this company may have had a more open and progressive attitude towards mental health issues whereas I have spoken with friends who tell a very different tale. For me, it only had a positive impact, so much so I wondered why every one of us, whether we're the CEO or the newbie, couldn't just allow ourselves to be vulnerable and real more often. Wouldn't we get so much more done? Wouldn't the quality of our work improve?

In my willingness to be vulnerable, I enjoyed a better connection with my boss and wanted to work harder for her, which could only have been a positive for the company. I produced better work because I felt more comfortable and the weight of trying to pretend that I am permanently unflappable was lifted. By addressing it, I could then park it and continue to do my job knowing that it was OK if I was not OK sometimes. It wasn't a secret I had to bury.

Because of this, I started feeling more resilient and far less anxious day-to-day. I realised that just because I am a sensitive person, does not mean I am any less capable of doing my job, and neither is she. I can still achieve great things in spite of my vulnerability. Eventually, I would be able to say that I could achieve great things *because* of my vulnerability.

If you look to a traditional, high-pressure corporate environment, for example, where vulnerability would have been (and in some cases might still be) discouraged, I struggle to identify any positive, long-term outcomes on you as an individual – or for the company, being honest – as a result of this way of living or working. Sure, there might be some short-term benefits: you give a great first impression, you get the job, you seem to have it all figured out, you get through the day, you get the work done, you land a big client (or whatever the equivalent might be in your field), you avoid the potentially awkward conversation of articulating how you really feel, and having people realise there is actual blood coursing through your body. People think you're great at what you do and that 'nothing fazes you' but then you go home and realise you are not OK. You found that day tough. Things do faze you. You are trying to keep it together. If this isn't familiar to you, just watch *The Devil Wears Prada* and you'll know exactly what I'm talking about. Apparently, the film is not at all far from the reality on which it's based.

I've also spoken with friends who have very senior roles in corporate companies. One particular friend was the head honcho at a global digital-media company and though I knew her as a friend and not a boss, she found out that some of the junior staff members saw her as incredibly intimidating. Needless to say, this had a negative effect on her. She realised they didn't see her as a person, and this was not good. To them, she was an untouchable boss. She never showed her vulnerability at work for all the reasons we've been led to believe it's a bad idea, and it actually resulted in a disconnect between her and her team. They didn't feel they could approach her. They didn't believe she would relate to them, yet there she was, telling me about her own struggles, her imposter syndrome, her worrying about what the junior members thought of her. As I listened, I thought, *When there's no room for vulnerability, nobody wins.*

I acknowledge that it's easier for me to be vulnerable in my day-to-day life when I'm writing about these very topics, and I have had people ask me, for example, how someone might own their anxiety or reveal their vulnerability when they're a solicitor in the courtroom or some other profession where you're expected to maintain a constant state of being unflappable. It was a good point and it got me thinking: how can we allow for vulnerability at work without it compromising our professionalism?

The answer, I believe, lies in our perception of it. We're thinking of it as weakness and that it makes us unreliable. We're visualising the solicitor in this scenario as someone about to burst into tears while trying to negotiate the very serious terms of a couple's separation, for example. We're imagining the couple having a meeting with him while he butts in to tell them about the dramatics of his own divorce. We assume being vulnerable means we have to tell the whole world about how we're feeling and we also assume that to show vulnerability means to show sadness or fear or worry. I've heard people say something along the lines of: 'So, what now? Are we all supposed to wear our hearts on our sleeves and tell everyone when we're upset? Are we to go into work and cry and say we're scared and clueless?' Well, no, not exactly.

This is not what vulnerability is about. And it's these ideas that encourage the cynicism, the eye-rolling and the widespread snowflake rhetoric whenever vulnerability is mentioned. For me, contrary to the age-old definition, I see vulnerability quite simply as authenticity and enabling your humaneness to be present.

In that scenario, the solicitor, who is going through something similar to the couple, might say to them that he empathises, he knows it's hard. He might tell them he's been through a separation himself, without having to share the gory details, thus enabling a more authentic and meaningful connection with his clients. In relating to him better, his clients will trust him more too. They will see him as a human and not just as a solicitor, but they will also know he can draw from his own experience and still fulfil his role to the best of his ability. He has normalised his vulnerability, and will feel stronger for it.

If we go back to my head-honcho friend, she doesn't need to talk herself down or dredge up insecurities at a staff meeting just to make the junior staff feel better. When you're a boss, you have to be encouraging and reliable, but you can still be authentic. For example, in a staff meeting, she could bridge the gap between ultra-professional and more relatable by saying, 'I'm not well versed on this topic so can somebody else bring me up to speed?', offering that opportunity to the more junior members, rather than pretending she knows everything and then scrambling in the privacy of her office to fill herself in.

She could even instigate one-on-one catch-ups with each member of her team and in that more private environment could reveal that, when she was at their level, she was worried about X, Y or Z, or mention to them that it may seem that when you get to her level you'll have it all figured out but you're always learning and this is why she's surrounded herself with this particular team, etc.

These are all hypothetical examples but you get what I'm saying: you don't need to throw yourself on the office floor in a tantrum because you're upset about something – that would be inappropriate and unprofessional – but looking for natural moments of authenticity might seem like no big deal but will have a hugely positive impact on your experience at work.

Another irony of vulnerability I have found is that when you're willing to show it, vulnerability can serve as a clear sign of confidence. For example, I know that I am very often flying by the seat of my pants, or that I have no clue, as a freelancer, how I'll pay my bills from one month to the next. Saying this doesn't make me any less successful. I am confident that I cannot work myself into the ground without suffering the repercussions. But I am also confident of being hired by a company to talk to their staff about managing anxiety and telling the organisers and the staff that I still deal with it all the time, I'm not speaking from a position of authority where I've solved the Rubik's cube. I would never put that pressure on myself.

I am confident to say when things are too much for me, workwise or any-other-wise. Saying this doesn't make me any less capable. I'm confident that there are people far more knowledgeable on lots of things than me. Better writers. Better editors. Better speakers. I was happy to tell the world about my efforts to launch my books in America, despite the enormous unlikelihood of success given the size of the country, and how hard it is to make an impact there. I was confident in trying, even if it didn't work out. I didn't keep it all on the downlow for fear that if it all went awry, then I would appear unsuccessful or as though I had failed. All of these are vulnerabilities but owning them is confidence.

Let me give you a real-life example of the vulnerability paradox and the confidence that comes from it.

I recently interviewed Samantha Barry, editor-in-chief of the US edition of *Glamour* magazine, for an Irish magazine. She was only a few months into the new role and, straight off the bat, she had no qualms in admitting that she felt intensely vulnerable upon accepting this new role. I was already impressed by her achievements but this authenticity took her to a whole new level for me.

Coming from a social media and digital background (at CNN) into a predominantly print environment, and one that was hugely focused on fashion, there were plenty of 'gaps' in her knowledge that, needless to say, others in the industry – who perhaps were vying for the role – were only dying to point out. But rather than cover over these gaps and pretend they didn't exist, she owned her vulnerability from the get-go, allowing those who knew more in certain areas to show the way (one of the tell-tale signs of good leadership).

This had a number of positive outcomes: if she was willing to say she didn't know it all from day one, nobody could say it back to her or judge her for it (removing the possibility of attack: invulnerable). It meant that she could hone in on what she could and would bring to the table: her strengths in areas where *Glamour* needed more bite (showing true confidence). Though she didn't tell me this, I imagine it took the pressure from her, enabling her to be someone who was still a work in progress (allowing for self-acceptance and self-compassion) – something that, of course, we all are.

It meant her new team at *Glamour* saw her as a human being rather than a robot or someone unrelatable and intimidating, and this enabled better connection with her team. This meant that they too would feel less pressure to have everything figured out all of the time and, as a result, would work in a more collaborative and creative manner (a positive domino effect on others), leaning into each other's strengths and not being afraid to ask for help where it was needed. Asking for help was not identifying a weakness, instead the willingness to ask was highlighting a strength. For Samantha Barry, owning her vulnerability turned out to be among her greatest strengths.

The more I look at vulnerability, the more I realise that a fear of it is what drives a lot of our anxieties. For example, in relationships, a fear of revealing our true selves keeps us from getting close to the person we want to let in. A fear of what people think of us adds a huge amount of weight to any general anxiety we're experiencing. And if we take something like imposter syndrome, which so many of us fall victim to, I would say that a fear of vulnerability is why you feel like an imposter in the first place.

If this fear of vulnerability lies at the root of so many of our personal issues, then it makes sense to me that a willingness to be vulnerable is also the antidote.

Take imposter syndrome, for example: the uneasy feeling that what you put out to the world is hugely at odds with how you view yourself privately. To stop feeling like an imposter, you introduce who you really are to the world – including your vulnerability – and instantly, your imposter identity evaporates and what's left is authenticity. You bridge the gap between your private self and public self, and so imposter anxiety is no longer an issue.

We've long been terrified of vulnerability but if you can stop and take a moment to get acquainted with it, you'll soon realise it holds the key to not just relieving you of these common anxieties, but bringing you to a place of ease.

Another important note on vulnerability. It's not just about owning our anxieties or insecurities or the things that we perceive to be 'weaknesses', it's also about owning our confidence. For me, showing my confidence, speaking up, being proud of myself, patting myself on the back, celebrating my achievements big and small can all also require a willingness to be vulnerable. Why? Because, unfortunately, at least in Ireland where I live and work, showing confidence can leave you open to judgement, which you might describe as a form of attack if you go back to the original dictionary definition of vulnerability.

Why the judgement? Because, for too long, confidence has been perceived as arrogance. The who-does-she-think-she-is response, of which I myself have been guilty, springs to mind.

Confidence isn't always warmly received, especially when it comes to women – self-deprecation and humility is preferred and celebrated – and, as such, it's easier to hide your confidence and dumb down your successes and accomplishments in order to be accepted and avoid the backlash. In some ways, it might be even easier to reveal the bad stuff because, as a society, we're more comfortable with that, it makes us feel more accepting of our own insecurities.

Someone's confidence, though it should inspire, threatens the insecure status quo. Think about it: we love it when a celebrity tells us about a time they felt as though they weren't up to the job. But when they say: 'I knew I was the right person for this role and never for a moment doubted myself', we tend to think, *Well, they certainly think a lot of themselves*, as if that's a bad thing. To put the good stuff out there is therefore an act of owning our vulnerability too. But remember: It's not about saying you're confident when you don't feel it, and it's not about wallowing in the more insecure parts of your experience, it's about being authentic and real.

I'm on good terms with vulnerability these days. But for a long time, things were a bit icy between us. I've resisted it my whole life. I didn't want to know about it. I always tried to be someone I'm not in order to fit in: the person who wanted to go to festivals and slam shots and sleep in a soggy tent (which is my idea of hell), the person who could travel to some far-flung corner of the world at a moment's notice with no real concern for things like 'traveller's diarrhoea' (again, my idea of hell and a concern that's always *top* of my list). I tried not to be anxious, but I was. I tried not to have tummy issues, but I did. I tried to fit in with peers who were maturing faster than I was ready for, but I didn't.

And when, eventually, my anxiety got the better of me, I was petrified. Not just because of the anxiety itself but what it might say about me, or how others might perceive me: I was afraid that I would seem weak, unemployable, undateable, incapable. For so long, I pushed against it, hoping desperately that if I just pretended that I was fine, then I would be.

The fear of vulnerability and the resistance to my anxiety and my reality at the time bubbled over, spilling like green acid from a witch's cauldron, souring everything in its path. But when I started to own it, first with myself and then with the rest of the world (which was my coping mechanism), I disarmed the vulnerability. I lessened the anxiety. I empowered myself. I increased my confidence. I made myself feel, as per the paradox, invulnerable. And I did that by choosing authenticity above all else.

Before you go applying vulnerability to your daily life, you have to start working on your perception of it. You have to accept that we've all been conditioned to abandon our vulnerability as a coping mechanism in adulthood but know that it's something you can change. It will require a shift in perspective, something that won't be possible without the carving out of new neural pathways, which we know from Chapter 2 won't happen overnight, so we've got to be patient. And start practising vulnerability in small, doable steps.

Expressing vulnerability at work might be two steps too soon, but a great and necessary place to start with vulnerability is in a relationship, especially if you've been hiding from it in recent years. The success of a romantic relationship will depend on the willingness of both parties to be vulnerable. Without it, you won't build intimacy. Without it, you won't build trust and you won't have the confidence to know that they love you for all that you are, not just the bits you'd advertise on your Tinder profile. A relationship without vulnerability cannot expect longevity. If you're not in a romantic relationship, you can still do this with a friend. It might be less intense with a friendship, but vulnerability shared between two friends will reap the same rewards of closeness, trust and empathy. Not only will your relationship benefit but you as individuals will benefit from feeling accepted, supported and worthy of love or friendship.

It helps to first consider why you're reluctant to show vulnerability in the first place. Are you afraid of being judged? What is the worst that can happen? If you do open up in a relationship and it doesn't yield the results you'd hoped for, you have to ask yourself if it's a good relationship for you to be in. Maybe your fears around vulnerability are warranted, maybe you won't get the support you need. In the right relationship there will be ample room for vulnerability when you're willing to show it.

I find it also helps to start by articulating how you feel for yourself. Before you share your vulnerability with someone else, explore it with yourself. How would you put it into words? Whether you express it on paper or simply muse in the bath, this is really worth doing to ensure that what you're saying doesn't get miscommunicated.

For example, I remember when I started going out with Barry, I wanted him to know that I wasn't sure I was ready for something serious. I had just come out of a long-term relationship and was afraid of committing again so soon because I was only starting to feel good again. I felt pressure to be in this new relationship but it wasn't coming from Barry, it was coming from me. And so I had to formulate my thoughts and really figure out where my vulnerability was coming from before I shared it with him, otherwise it might all come out wrong and it might sound to him as though I just wasn't interested in him when really it was more of a timing issue for me. It might also have sounded like I was insinuating that he was pressuring me when, again, this was not the case.

I felt more confident about sharing my feelings when I had taken some time to accept them for myself. When I told him, he understood. He appreciated my honesty and he also empathised with my fears around not wanting to be hurt again. With this the pressure instantly went away, and I was able to then spend time with him and be my authentic self. He was fully aware of where we stood and, before long, we were deeply connected. We're now a boring old married couple (and happy about it too).

Recap: Before sharing vulnerability in a relationship, ask yourself the following:

o Why am I reluctant to show my vulnerability?

○ What do I fear will happen if I do?
○ How would I respond to my partner sharing their vulnerability – would I want them to?
○ How can I best articulate my vulnerability?

When you are ready to act on your vulnerability in a relationship, it helps to start by saying what you really think about something and catch yourself when you automatically jump to say what you think sounds better, which is something you might do in the early days of getting to know someone. Sharing with your partner that there's a goal you really want to reach for and that you think you might actually be able to pull it off is an act of sharing vulnerability.

Another key way to introduce vulnerability in a relationship is to ask for what you need. This can be scary but it's worth doing. For example, I'll sometimes say to Barry if I'm having an anxious wave that I'd really like it if he could stay in with me in the evening and cancel his plans so that I'm not alone feeling poorly. This goes against the how-to-be-a-super-cool-laid-back-girlfriend rule book but fuck it, it's real.

I do any and all of these things in my marriage but also with my friends. I'd do it with the postman and the butcher and the person who stubs my ticket at the train station too, but that's probably not necessary.

Here are some vulnerability and authenticity alternative examples that could be relevant at the beginning of a relationship or when you've been in one for a while:

o commit to your own opinions even if they won't be shared
o ask for what you need
o notice when you're trying to appear laid back and are concealing how you really feel
o tell them about a time that you doubted yourself or some other past vulnerable experience
o start a conversation about things you are both afraid of.

Why do I encourage you to own your vulnerability in all aspects of your life and not just your relationships? Because this will merge you with your authentic self and, when you do that, very little can really damage you. It's a very powerful place to be.

In my professional life, it took the pressure off me hugely. I'd say things such as, 'Here's what I know I can do and here's what I know I can't do or don't have much experience in' or 'You know, I've done enough of this now to know that this is a major strength of mine, I really think I'm right for this'. It opens you up to greater opportunities, and makes you far more resilient to the missed opportunities too.

Vulnerability might sometimes feel like 'weakness', it might feel like a risk, and showing it might feel like you're doing yourself a disservice, but owning it is anything but. It's the freedom to be who you are, how you are, as you are, when you are, without resisting or denying it to yourself, whether it's good or bad, positive or negative, whether you're proud of yourself and confident or unsure of yourself and out of your depth. And whether or not you want to vocalise it to others is your choice. The most important thing is owning it for yourself at the very least. Because when you allow yourself to be vulnerable, you become invulnerable.

 PAUSE FOR THOUGHT

Vulnerability is not something to avoid, it's something to gravitate towards and to own. Stop thinking of vulnerability in the traditional sense, as though you will be under threat by revealing how vulnerable you are, and start to reimagine it as authenticity.

Find opportunities for authenticity as you go through your day. Watch as others respond in kind. Prove me wrong that a willingness to own vulnerability doesn't make you feel as though you are in fact invulnerable. If I haven't succeeded in convincing you by now that it's no longer a dirty word or something you need to hide behind, I'll borrow from the wise words of Brené Brown to wrap up. 'Vulnerability is not winning or losing; it's having the courage to show up and be seen when we have no control over the outcome. Vulnerability is not weakness; it's our greatest measure of courage.'

She's not wrong.

Truth #6
Not everyone will like you

TIME FOR THE TRUTH about people-pleasing and how to do less of it.

At this point in the book, we're going to sink our teeth into one of the most commonly experienced and self-imposed drivers of anxiety there is: people-pleasing. If you simply Google the phrase 'people-pleaser' you will find that, just like imposter syndrome, it's the 'anxiety du jour' that grips many a millennial. We've got yet another emotional epidemic on our hands, one that, until we identify it within ourselves, we might not even be aware of.

Picture this: I'm sat in the salon chair, watching my freshly dyed hair dry to what can only be described as Barney the dinosaur purple – far removed from the Instagrammable auburn tones I had requested in the first place. However, I nod and smile as the hairdresser says with gusto, 'This is just gorgeous!' I hated it (at that moment I hated her too), and though I know it's only hair and, yes, there are more important things in life, I wanted to cry. Staring at my reflection in the mirror, I then entered a silent battle with my people-pleasing self. Weighing things up, I figured I would simply pretend that I was happy, pay the extortionate 240 euro, plus tip, lest they think I was a tight-arse. I could then go home, sob and then book somewhere else to get it fixed. This would be far easier than the alternative which would require me to be honest and say, 'I don't like it.'

Admit I wasn't happy? No way!

This would mean disappointing the girl who had spent a long time on what she figured was a job well done. Saying I wanted to have it fixed there and then would mean messing up their appointment schedule for the remainder of the day and that added stress would be on me. I'd probably hurt the girl's feelings too. She would definitely think badly of me (or so I thought) and despite the fact that I would never go back to that salon and would be unlikely to bump into this complete stranger, I couldn't cope with the thought of someone - anyone! - not liking me or having a bad impression of me.

I imagined her, later on with her colleagues, discussing what a difficult client I'd been. So far, being honest about how I felt seemed to come with far too great a risk in the short term. Going home with shit hair (as well as being down 240 euro) was worth it if it meant avoiding this uncomfortable social interaction.

So, what did I do?

We'll get to that in just a moment (I know, the suspense must be killing you), but in the meantime, if this sort of situation sounds at all familiar, then I hate to break it to you: like me, you are a people-pleaser and it's precisely this type of seemingly innocuous, everyday experience that encouraged me to write this particular chapter. That and getting whacked in the boob by the grocery bag of someone rushing past me on the street and somehow believing that I'm the one who should apologise.

I wanted to understand how people-pleasing works, why we engage in this very frustrating behaviour (and why we have done since the beginning of time). I wanted to look at how it really affects us, as well as, crucially, offering a solution – or at the very least a series of practical options – that will help us to navigate these murky waters and enable us to start to put our own needs first.

It is believed that Virginia Satir, the family therapist, psychologist and author, originally coined the phrase 'people-pleaser'. In her view: 'a people-pleaser often feels that they have no value except for what they can do or be for another person'.

Clinical psychologist Jennifer Guttman refers to the more universally accepted definition of a people-pleaser as 'a person who has an emotional need to please others, often at the expense of his or her own needs or desires', while you'll also find people-pleasing described as a behaviour you engage in when you decide to discard your authenticity in order to become who you think others want or need you to be.

Before you go beating yourself up about it, know that, by and large, we all like to please others and, in our defence, we do it for good reason.

First of all, it's nice! We like to be liked. That's nice too. We tend not to gravitate towards conflict and we acknowledge that letting someone down is not a nice feeling. Again, all normal: who loves conflict?

For some of us, our people-pleasing tendencies are nothing more than a nuisance. We tend to be agreeable, we move and shift where necessary to avoid confrontation. We're yes people. We're reliable. According to various studies, our brain's reward centre lights up, giving us a nice spike in dopamine, from the simple act of pleasing someone else and being on the receiving end of their approval. Compliments, positive feedback and approval are things we crave.

Sound familiar? Oh, me too. So far, people-pleasing doesn't sound so bad. In fact, you might argue that there are worse things afflicting the human mind.

The thing is, while people-pleasing has some positive aspects to it and some short-term benefits – for example, making someone else's day a bit easier or avoiding an awkward conversation – it can have quite the ugly, long-term underbelly, which we'll soon be exploring. *New York Times* bestselling author and clinical psychologist Harriet Braiker was so concerned about our collective tendencies to people-please that she described it as a rather sinister-sounding psychological condition: 'the disease to please'.

For Braiker, and for me, our people-pleasing behaviours can veer into toxic territory if we're not careful. They can become a compulsion. A complete inability to say no to something we don't like or want to do. A people-pleasing-paralysis that stops us from asserting ourselves, saying what we really think, what we really like and what we would really prefer to do. An endless and insatiable craving for others' approval – even those we don't personally know – that can never fulfil us.

This might sound extreme but, chances are, you'll find yourself somewhere on this spectrum between automatically putting others' needs before your own and losing the plot entirely when disappointing someone is something you can't avoid.

Before we go about addressing it, we need to first understand why we are so obsessed with the idea of being liked and pleasing others' in the first place. There are a few reasons.

Jennifer Guttman says we engage in this behaviour to reduce our fears of abandonment. We're afraid of being left out, which, as we'll get to, has its roots in evolution.

What's more, Amy Morin, another clinical psychotherapist, believes that where people-pleasing is an issue, you'll typically find self-esteem/self-worth issues at play, namely our desire for external validation as a measure of how valuable we are. Rather than validate ourselves, which every self-help book you read will tell you to do, we have a tendency to allow others – externally – to do this for us. I know I actively seek out a sense of my own self-worth through the constant approval of others.

Unfortunately, our self-worth is too often wrapped up in what psychologists call an 'external validation mental model' and it's fair to say that social media, with all of its likes and shares and visual measures of popularity, has sent us further down the rabbit hole of external validation.

While social media has certainly exacerbated it, a 2016 study in *Psychological Science* showed how the reward centres in teenagers' brains lit up by way of increased dopamine by simply looking at a social media post where they'd got lots of likes. We have long decided on the kind of person we are based on the feedback we receive from those around us. Their reactions to us and how we behave provide a mirror in which we can see our value. Dr Pamela Rutledge tells US magazine *SheKnows* that this need for social connection, which approval and popularity enables, has always been essential to our mental and physical health. 'Being liked reinforces our sense of self-esteem and affiliation. We should not feel bad for wanting others to like us. This is a common human motivation and is how social norms are established and reinforced.'

We've looked for confirmation of our value in this way since we were babies. Back in our cots, we literally looked to the facial expressions of our care-givers to assess whether or not we were approved of, loved and worthy or whether we were going to be rejected.

The reason we looked to others for validation as children was because we were not yet self-sufficient. Our well-being depended entirely on the love of our parents and those who looked after us to continue looking after us. Somewhere along the road to adulthood, we were supposed to start relying on ourselves to determine our self-worth, swapping external validation for internal validation, but I think it's fair to say that quite a few of us missed the memo on that one. I for one must have been off sick that day.

Behind this need for external validation, which people-pleasing affords us, you'll find a deep-seated, biologically conditioned imperative to survive. Yup, we really can partially blame evolution for so many of our more uncomfortable experiences today, from anxiety to our negativity bias, from jealousy to the fear that someone else's success would take from ours and, of course, people-pleasing.

I acknowledge that it starts to get a little bit repetitive – blaming our ancestors, how convenient! – but the truth is, the more I look at the 'why' behind certain behaviours, the more I come back to survival as their ultimate driving force.

In terms of people-pleasing, from what I understand, it was very important, back in the days of the Flintstones, that we were not just part of a social group (or a 'tribe') but that we got along with the others in it, had their approval and that they liked us. If we weren't a member of a tribe, we were alone, and nobody lasted very long alone out in the wilderness.

Among the many reasons why tribal life was necessary to our survival was that we needed community to create shelter and look after children while other members sought food and water. We needed a tribe in order to keep safe at night: certain people would take the first shift, keeping watch while others slept, and then they would switch roles at a certain point, meaning everybody got their opportunity to rest while always being looked after. In order to be part of this tribe, and for our tribe to function well, we had to be co-operative in our respective roles, in the same way we have to be co-operative in a working environment today. We had to adhere to what was expected of us. We had to please others and say yes. Doing this kept us safe and also made us feel good – remember the dopamine hit? If we failed to be co-operative or we were too focused on suiting ourselves, we'd have royally pissed off other members of the tribe. This would result in conflict and the likelihood of being pushed out of the group. If we weren't good enough at our jobs, we'd be criticised, further questioning our position in the group. If we were ousted by the group, we'd find ourselves alone again. From there, things would become very difficult, our chance of survival would nosedive, we'd experience a lot of fear and it wouldn't be long before we found ourselves resembling something akin to chopped liver.

For this reason, it was essential that we pleased those within our tribe; being liked increased our chance of survival. Going against the requests of our tribe or daring to say 'no' was far too great a risk. And, so, we evolved to be agreeable because it served our brain's primary role of keeping us alive exceptionally well.

In those more black-and-white, hunter-gatherer times, the choice was suiting ourselves or risking our lives, and, of course, the choice was easy; staying alive was the goal. The side-effects of people-pleasing – perhaps resentment towards other members of the tribe – were totally worth it if it meant getting through another day. Suffice it to say, the concept of 'you do you' was not a smart one in hunter-gatherer times.

Fast forward to today, however, and the once-legitimate threats to our physical survival have all but gone, certainly when it comes to people-pleasing. We've replaced the threat of physical survival with the threat of emotional survival – or rather, our emotional well-being. What has remained is our need for validation, as well as our fear of rejection and disapproval. What's more, we're still operating largely in tribes, be it our family, our group of friends, our sports team, our social media community or our team at work. And in those tribes, we still instinctively want to please others, because we want to be liked, because we want to survive.

It's in our nature to want to be inside the group, rather than outside of it, and so our brains reckon that being co-operative and agreeable is still the surest way of inoculating ourselves against these risks. As such, we please everyone from the postman to the charity mugger to our boss. And it works! People are appeased, you stay in their good books, you stay in the tribe, and you're still intact.

The short-term benefits of people-pleasing are obvious. It's much easier to do it than not to do it.

You avoid conflict.

You avoid an uncomfortable social encounter.

You avoid disappointing others.

You bolster your reliability (particularly at work).

And because we're more conditioned to do what suits us best in the here and now, with less focus on our future selves, we continue to people-please on autopilot.

If we go against this in the short term, it immediately creates a conflict that our minds and bodies do not like. We are pushing back against our nature - because people-pleasing is linked to our survival - and we're likely to come up against conflict both internally and externally. Internally we feel guilty, we feel tension. Externally, someone might react badly to us when we say no. They might write us off or exclude us. They might dislike us. We have a threat to our emotional survival that feels immediate.

It's really only when you remove the life-or-death pressure from our daily experience, as is the case today, that the more negative effects of people-pleasing become apparent. Today, saying no or disappointing someone doesn't come with the same high-stakes risk and so we're left with yet another survival-instinct hangover. One that no longer serves us all that well and one that we're trying, yet struggling, to change.

The long-term downsides to people-pleasing are harder to identify, as they take time to build up. Here's how I see it: while saying no or suiting ourselves might feel like a threat to our emotional survival in the here and now, the alternative of consistently pleasing others will slowly become a threat to our emotional survival in the long run. Over time, it threatens our whole sense of well-being.

Let's take a quick look at the main culprits, shall we?

○ stress, depression and anxiety
○ passive aggression and resentfulness towards others
○ loss of integrity and authenticity
○ inability to cope with confrontation
○ unsure of your own likes/tastes/interests
○ target of exploitation
○ perpetuating your need for external validation and lack of self-worth
○ compromised health and well-being
○ neglected self.

Yikes, seriously? It's this bad?

It can be.

According to Dr Sherry Pagoto, Professor in the Department of Allied Health Sciences at the University of Connecticut, when writing about people-pleasing for *Psychology Today*, we will likely feel one or several of these.

A very common one, she says, is passive aggression towards those who we are constantly pleasing. We're doing things we don't really want to do to suit others, and so we feel resentful of them. With ourselves, we might get frustrated at the loss of our own integrity. We might even find it hard to enjoy other people and activities. We'll find ourselves emotionally fatigued, perhaps depressed and stressed out from pleasing everybody else ahead of us.

Pagoto explains that we might also find ourselves being taken advantage of. You start out enjoying the idea that you are reliable, but will soon find that you've become a target for exploitative behaviour. Another side-effect is that we're not even sure what it is we want to do anymore, we're so used to doing what we think we should be doing, which means our sense of self is compromised. We certainly don't feel authentic in how we engage with others in the world. We continue to rely on pleasing others as a way to measure our self-worth, we don't give ourselves the chance to move away from external validation.

Overall, Pagoto blames excessive people-pleasing for a neglected self. We're so concerned with nourishing others above ourselves that we put ourselves at greater risk of health problems. 'Wanting to take care of others is not a bad thing and if more people had a little bit of what you have, the world would be a better place,' explains Pagoto. 'However, you cannot do this at the expense of yourself. A balance is needed. Consider that taking care of yourself makes you better equipped to take care of others by giving you the energy and vitality to do it even better than you are now. Imagine you are driving a Red Cross truck delivering food and water to hurricane victims. If you are in such a hurry to get to every single victim that you don't stop once in a while to refuel the truck, eventually you will be stalled on the side of the road helping no one. Think of the time you put into exercise, de-stressing and eating healthy as your fuel stops.'

What's more, we get so used to pleasing others and avoiding conflict that when we inevitably find ourselves in a confrontational situation – it's bound to happen at some stage or another, especially in a professional environment – we cannot cope.

All in all, you might be starting to realise that people-pleasing isn't quite the convenient social tool you once thought it was. You might also be starting to think that maybe your long-term emotional survival and well-being is worth more to you than enduring one potentially uncomfortable moment in which you decide to be authentic about what you do and do not want to do, when you assert yourself and say, 'No, that's not for me.'

You're ready to stop people-pleasing but going against what comes naturally to you is not easy. Where do you start? To get to a place where you can at least choose between pleasing others and pleasing yourself (rather than always automatically opting for the former), you must start with the baptism of fire that is our next blunt truth ...

Not everyone will like you.

Yes, it's a tough one, but here's the thing – even if you people-please to the nth degree to avoid having anybody ever think poorly of you, the hard truth is that there will always be people who dislike you, people who get a bad first impression of you or those who simply take you up the wrong way.

If this is a given, you may as well start suiting yourself more often, right?

In a way it's liberating. There will be people who don't like what you do, don't like what you're about or what you say, so you may as well do you. There will be people who don't like your outfits or don't like the sound of your voice. There will even be people – hopefully not many – who consider you the villain in one of their stories. Everyone has been, or will someday be, a villain in somebody else's story, but this doesn't necessarily mean you're a bad person.

Even if this was the greatest book ever written and hailed as such, I can guarantee you I could still go digging into the abyss of

Amazon reviews and find those who would rather have watched paint dry than to read it. You'll never be 'for' everyone, you'll never be everyone's cup of tea, and when you start to accept and surrender to this universal truth, changing your people-pleasing behaviours becomes an awful lot easier.

I say this because, in my experience, it's this paralysing desire to be liked that seems to drive my own people-pleasing tendencies.

So that's step one. Not everyone will like you and you are OK with that. Your survival will not be at risk because someone doesn't like you.

Step two? We need to talk about our fear of how badly our decision to honour our own needs will be received.

Will the world come crashing down on us? Will the person hate us? Reject us? Freak out at us? This, I find, is mostly our perception of what might happen and if I've learned anything, it's that our perceptions, especially those of anxious overthinkers like me, rarely measure up with reality.

In the case of people-pleasing, this is good news. We are often so afraid not to people-please for the reasons mentioned above but, in my experience, it almost never pans out the way we suspect it will when we suit ourselves. The risk in our head is far greater than the risk in real life.

Why is this? In my opinion, it is because we consistently overestimate our importance in the lives of others. I don't mean that in a you're-not-important-to-other-people kind of way, but, in general, we are all far too concerned with what's going on in our own lives and in our own heads to devote too much time to analyse someone else's actions.

We give far too much weight to how we think other people will react when, in reality, they might simply react with a jolt of disappointment - they might go so far as to voice their disappointment, but then they will move on, back to worrying about how they're coming across to others or how they're faring in their own tribe.

Think about how you've responded when somebody has said no to you. Of course, it will depend on the situation and the reason why they are saying no - if something terrible has happened and they have to opt out you wouldn't bat an eyelid, but you might feel a pang of disappointment, if, say, they're saying no because they're not interested. I know I have felt this in the past, but do you exit the conversation thinking badly of them? As long as they were honest and kind in their delivery, then no, you don't.

If someone does come away disliking you as a result or handles it very badly, this honestly says more about them than it does about you. And you're back to the truth that sometimes, some people just won't like you, and they're certainly not the people you should be going out of your way to please.

The best thing that can happen – and what's far more likely if you think about how you would react – is that the other person will understand, value your reasoning and carry on. And though they might not be aware of it, they'll probably have a lot of respect for you and your ability to set your own terms, wishing they had the courage to do the same. It is what is needed for us to carve out the neural pathway that enables us to stop and think, *Is this really something I want to do?*

We need to learn to accept how prone we can be to overestimating our importance and the effect of our behaviour on others. We need to realise just how much of the turmoil associated with not people-pleasing is self-generated and wrapped up in anticipation, and at the absolute worst, if our fears are realised, we need to learn to get comfortable with the idea of disappointing someone once in a while. If that happens, we need to be prepared for the possibility that this person will voice their disappointment to us, which might be uncomfortable, but I find this to be a rare occurrence: when you've said no in a way that is kind, considerate and explains your motivation for saying no in the first place, you'll get the reaction you were hoping for.

At this point I want to remind you of Dr Kelly McGonigal's wise words covered in Chapter 2. Bring your future self into your mind's eye when considering your actions in the here and now. Remember to call on your 'I want' power, which will help to keep you thinking of the bigger picture and what you really want for yourself in general as opposed to what is easiest at the moment. Do you want to compromise your well-being by always putting others' needs before your own? Nope.

Let's circle back to the salon chair. By the time I found myself in that scenario, I had already begun researching this particular topic, questioning my behaviour and wanting to test the waters of what would happen if, God forbid, I chose not to be a people-pleaser just once. I was a customer, I wasn't happy, they would want to know if their customer wasn't happy because surely customer satisfaction is a priority of theirs, and let's not forget the fact that I was about to hand over a large sum of money.

So, when she asked me, 'What do you think?'

I paused, attempted to steel myself, and said, 'It's not quite what I was expecting.'

She said, 'OK.' No apology.

I continued, 'I'm sorry, it just looks a little bit purple to me?'

Again, she said, 'OK.' But I knew she was disagreeing with me in her head.

Of course, she'd rather not have to deal with a dissatisfied customer, that can't ever be fun.

She then said we could go back to the sink, lift the toner (the blatantly purple toner) out of my hair and then go in with another, more auburn, toner.

I said, 'Thank you. If you don't mind?'

And she rinsed my hair once more.

I honestly lost count of the amount of times I said, 'I'm really sorry about this' or something to that effect. I was trying desperately to save myself, in a roundabout way, from all of the risks that would come with suiting myself but, in apologising profusely for my honesty, I pretty much undid the bravery of my initial declaration of dissatisfaction.

I realised that while I was starting to pause between stimulus and automatic people-pleasing behaviour, which was a positive step forward, whenever I succeeded in putting myself first, I turned to apologetic language as some kind of lifeboat to rescue me from the fear of being disliked.

This was another roadblock.

I was still believing that the number-one priority was to be liked and that by suiting myself, I would immediately be disliked. In being apologetic – such as saying sorry in an email when you're looking for something from a co-worker – I wasn't guaranteed the outcome I'd hoped for, I was merely undermining myself and my value.

Couldn't I say I wasn't happy without saying sorry at the same time? I had done nothing wrong. Couldn't I send an email to a client who was late on paying my invoice, which I needed in order to pay my bills, without saying sorry for the fact that I'm looking for what I was owed? If anyone's going to be apologising, shouldn't it be the person who is six months late on paying me? Shouldn't it be the girl who made an epic balls of my hair?

When we are consistently apologetic in how we communicate with others, we start to believe that we are in the way, that we are a nuisance, that we are bothering others, that we are not as important. We believe that we have to apologise for taking care of ourselves. We believe that we are not worthy of being pleased ahead of anyone else.

As you can imagine, this doesn't help to bolster our self-worth. And while it might seem like you are being compassionate towards others, you're definitely not showing any compassion towards yourself, which we now know increases our stress levels.

For me, apologetic behaviour had become my nice-girl default, a salve to make suiting myself that bit easier. 'I'm sorry to disturb you ...' is a common one. Another example of this can be something as simple as the word 'just' in your email correspondence.

'I'm just emailing to see if you got my invoice.'

'I just wanted to check if you were available.'

Though it's one small, seemingly innocent word, 'just', when used in this way, is unnecessarily apologetic. If you think about it, the word 'just' alone has the power to please – or at least appease – people and make you appear deferential at the same time. As though you have to open with an apology or a justification to make what you're about to say easier for the person on the receiving end to digest.

It's similar to writing 'sorry about this, but ...' It instantly places you in a subservient position to the person you are emailing and it puts you and your needs down.

I noticed myself doing this a lot a few years ago and decided that I would never use the word 'just' in an email where it wasn't totally necessary. Instead of writing: 'I'm just emailing to see if you are free', for example, I would write: 'I wonder if you might be free' or 'How are you fixed?'

If you're looking for a good starting point with curbing your own people-pleasing behaviours, email is great because you have the time to gather your thoughts and the space to tailor your language. You can still be polite and friendly in how you communicate with others without automatically placing yourself on the back foot.

Most people want to be nice, kind and friendly towards others but this does not have to mean you're a people-pleaser. There is a big difference between being kind, which we should all aim to be because it makes the world a better place, and being a people-pleaser. We can learn to say no, be honest about how we feel and suit ourselves in a way that is still kind and never rude or hurtful to others. Working on your people-pleasing tendencies does not mean you are suddenly brusque, cold, inconsiderate or selfish. Not at all. It's just that you start to value yourself, your needs and what works for you and what doesn't with the same enthusiasm that you've been valuing everyone else's needs.

How to suit yourself

OK, now it's time to get practical. Let's start with saying no.

1. Create a temporary buffer

First of all, you need to create a buffer between being asked or offered something and actually responding, to ensure that you don't just say yes because it's easier in the moment. For example, saying something like 'That sounds great, let me get back to you' or 'I have a lot on so let me check how I'm fixed'.

Even if you know off the bat that you're going to say no, employing this buffer makes it easier because you give yourself the space to craft a response that you feel good about, as well as giving you the option of saying no via email or text if doing this in person is too much of a stretch for you.

2. Do not apologise but do say thank you

It should be obvious now but apologising should not be relied upon to make suiting yourself easier. You have nothing to apologise for and you'll do yourself a disservice by saying sorry.

Sometimes, we don't say sorry because we feel apologetic but because saying sorry sounds friendly and kind. What also sounds friendly and kind is saying thank you. So, I would always wrap a no in a thank you. 'Thanks for thinking of me, but I've got too much on.'

You also don't always have to be telling the truth, if, for example, the truth is you just couldn't be arsed. Saying that might not go down so well, so opt for softer language such as 'it doesn't suit'. 'Thanks so much for the invitation, but I'm going to sit this one out.'

Blunt truths should be reserved for close friends, where you can afford to be a little more direct. One of my best friends recently asked if I wanted her to add me to a new WhatsApp group she was setting up that shared daily inspiration and mindfulness objectives. I replied saying: 'I love you but I'm going to say no, I do not need any more digital distractions right now.' If close friends are getting together last minute, and I just don't feel like leaving my couch, I will say: 'Girls, I'm exhausted. I think I need a night at home to reset my batteries, but would love to catch up with you in the next week if that suits?' Offering an alternative also helps.

3. Close the loop

When debating whether or not to say no, or how to say no, we can sometimes end up leaving it too long before confirming one way or another and this, I believe, can be indirectly rude and inconsiderate.

You're always best off closing the loop, enduring the moment of potential disappointment from the other person and then allowing both you and them to move on. If you know you don't want to go on a group trip and you're avoiding committing or not committing until the last minute, it's this kind of behaviour that might actually create the outcome you'd most feared.

I think most people appreciate knowing where they stand sooner rather than later and nothing feels more disappointing than being told no at the last minute when you've suspected all along that they were always going to opt out.

When saying no, give yourself the initial buffer so as not to say the wrong thing, but then act on it; rip the band-aid off and then the hard part is done.

4. Be solution-focused

If I revisit the salon experience, what I could have said, rather than apologise profusely and dig myself into a hole, was, 'I know you've worked really hard on this but it's not what I wanted. Is there anything we can do to bring it closer to what I was hoping for?' or 'Now that it's drying, I think it's come out too dark for me, is there anything we can do?'. I wouldn't have to say 'I hate it, this is not what I asked for', I could express my customer dissatisfaction while at the same time being pleasant and respectful of the girl who'd done the job. By asking what we might do to rectify the situation, I come across more solution-focused than just plain pissed off.

In a restaurant situation where I'm not happy with the food and know I'll be kicking myself for paying the bill when I had my chance to complain, I'll say something like 'Thank you [for coming over to our table] but this is a little colder than I'd like, could you heat it up?' You don't have to say, 'I'm sorry but this is just a little bit too cold, sorry!' The former is far more empowering and fair while still kind and friendly.

Watch out for the word 'just', remove it wherever it's not entirely necessary and I guarantee it will be a game-changer for you.

If I'm chasing an invoice from a client who is late to pay me, I consciously replace: 'Hi there, I just wanted to check in and see if that payment might be processed soon?' or 'Sorry to chase but I was just wondering if that might go through soon?', with: 'Hi there, I wanted to follow up on that invoice. Do you need anything else from my end in order to process that payment? Thanks so much, have a great day.' Do you see the difference? If I open with the former, I'm basically identifying myself as a nuisance and something that will disrupt their day when, in reality, I am owed money for work already completed.

I could tell you so many of my own people-pleasing stories but here's a particular pickle worth sharing from a while back. A fashion designer with whom I'm vaguely familiar reached out to me and said that they would love to design something for me to wear, on the off-chance I had any events coming up.

I pushed back, telling them I was very grateful but I didn't think I had the social status they'd be looking for with which to associate their work. They insisted, saying they really wanted to and it would be their pleasure. So, I said OK!

They asked me what styles I liked and, because I wasn't a paying customer, I told them to please design whatever they thought would work for me. I didn't want to put demands on them when they were doing this for me! I also couldn't imagine ever saying I wasn't happy with it, if it came to that, because they had been so kind and generous in the first place.

But then they came to my house to take my measurements and though everything had been via email until now, as they left they said, 'It'll be €300 for the fabric, if that's okay? I won't make anything out of this myself but that will just cover the costs.'

I said, 'Yep, sure no problem at all!'

I then closed the door as the realisation hit me. I didn't need this outfit. I didn't have €300 to spare for something that wasn't an essential purchase. I didn't even have any events coming up where I could wear it! But I had gone along with it because I wanted to be nice and now I found myself facing a €300 bill.

How would I get out of this one? Especially now that I'd said it wasn't a problem.

In my defence, I'd been put in an unfair position. They had dropped the costs on me in person and neglected to tell me there would be a cost from the get-go. If they had said I'd need to pay €300 when they offered to make something, I would have told them that I appreciated that they thought of me, but that I needed to save every penny I had for an upcoming trip.

Also, saying it in person, and reminding me that they would make no money themselves in this exchange, made me feel guilty. Of course, I don't want someone to do something for free for me, but I had tried to say no and they had insisted, so I felt it was rude not to!

To my shame, it was a long time before I addressed this issue, out of fear and discomfort that you'll no doubt understand by now. What I should have done was said something like, 'Oh, I'm sorry [an apology is OK in this instance], I should have double-checked with you about costs. Of course I do not want you to be spending your own money to make this happen but, unfortunately, I can't pay that myself right now. I really appreciate you reaching out to me and I'd love to work together in the future but perhaps it's best to hold off for now?'

Sure, it would have been awkward, but I would have done both of us a favour. Failing that, I should have followed up with a message later that day saying: 'Listen, thanks so much for calling over, I really appreciate your time. You mentioned the €300 material cost as you were leaving and I was caught off-guard. I'm really sorry but I don't have that money right now and I certainly don't want this coming out of your own pocket, so maybe we should put the brakes on until I have an event and the budget to go with it?'

But I did neither of these things. And too much time has passed now, and no doubt they do think poorly of me for ghosting them, which I deserve. In trying so hard to avoid disappointing this person and failing to close the loop, I achieved nothing more than pissing them off, leaving them hanging and making myself feel foolish and embarrassed all at once.

In this case, saying no upfront would have saved me a lot of social anguish. Though I wouldn't recommend handling something the way I did, the result did teach me a valuable lesson and reminded me of our central truth: sometimes, try as you might to avoid it, you are going to fuck up, you're going to disappoint someone and, though you mean well, not everyone will like you.

How to react when others suit themselves

Before we close this chapter, I want to take a moment to think about this whole 'you do you' concept.

For many, it has become a mantra; something we find far easier to say than to actually execute. The thing is, we're all for 'you do you' with others, as long as it doesn't have an impact on us. What I mean here is that we're fine with people suiting themselves, as long as their suiting themselves suits us too.

I know this to be true from my own experience, when a friend has said no to me and I've wound up feeling disappointed and mistaking their attempts at suiting themselves for nothing more than selfishness. I remember having a conversation with a friend about a potential trip to New York. She sounded very enthused about the idea. I was going anyway for some work stuff, so I went home later that day and did what I thought was something nice: I booked flights for her to join me. I then told her what I'd done and rather than squeal with excitement, which I had hoped she would, she seemed really uncomfortable and said she'd have to 'see how she's fixed'. Needless to say, I was very upset. I think I actually cried. I thought, *How could she respond like this?* and I'm pretty sure I gave her the silent treatment for a while too, which, as a thirty-one year old, was not one of my finest moments.

But then, after a few days, when I spoke to her about it a little bit more, I saw things from her perspective. Maybe what I had done wasn't the kind gesture I thought it was, maybe it was actually me being selfish because I wanted her to come with me, because that suited me, and I didn't think to ask her if that was what she really wanted to do and if she could realistically make it happen (these are not things she said to me but conclusions I came to myself).

She's the kind of person who likes to be in control, who hates surprises, who likes to weigh things up before committing – and I ignored all of that to suit myself. And, to be fair to her, it had only been a hypothetical conversation and who doesn't like the idea of a trip to New York?

I then put her in a position that she had not asked to be put in, where she felt huge pressure not to disappoint me or let me down, because she knew my intentions were good. She also felt under pressure financially because work had been quiet (she's freelance like me) and she was watching her spending very carefully. In what I thought was a nice gesture, I had actually ruined her night – she had been out having dinner with her boyfriend when I'd texted her – as I placed this unnecessary, awkward discomfort upon her. But she had been working on her own people-pleasing behaviours, as well as her boundaries, and so when she bravely responded to say that she wasn't sure if this was going to work, explaining all of the above in what could only be described as reasonable and very kind language, I reacted in exactly the way she feared I would. I was not just disappointed, I thought badly of her and I felt hurt. Because I was thinking about things only from my perspective.

You see it's all well and good working on our own behaviours when it comes to people-pleasing, but it's equally important to look at how we perceive it when we're the ones being said no to.

We need to not only get comfortable with the reality that we will, at some point, disappoint others, but that sometimes we will be the ones to be disappointed. And when that happens, we need to stop and think about our reaction. We need to question ourselves when we perceive somebody else's no as selfish. Maybe their no is the very same as the no you wish you'd been brave enough to say. Maybe their no isn't coming from a bad place – they don't want to disappoint or hurt you, anything but – but they're just trying to protect themselves from the stress that pleasing can bring upon us.

We're all just trying to do the right thing, and while it's wonderful to place so much attention on our own actions and behaviours, it's really important, I think, that we let other people suit themselves too.

 PAUSE FOR THOUGHT

With this chapter, I wanted to bring your attention towards incessant people-pleasing behaviours and the negative effects they may be having on you, as well as offering some practical ways to turn this behaviour around.

But while my focus has been on what we referred to at the outset as 'the disease to please', that's not to say that pleasing others is always a bad thing and you should suit yourself and only yourself from here on out. It's a very kind thing and it shows that you are compassionate and considerate and you think of others, you're definitely not selfish, and so sometimes pleasing others is OK. These are not bad traits to have at all. You just need to be careful about where this behaviour is really coming from and when it is going against you.

To know whether it's the good or bad kind of people-pleasing, you need to focus as much as you can on your intention. Why do you want to say yes to this person? Are you saying yes for their approval? Or do you just want to do something nice for someone? I find it helps to always consider whether your people-pleasing behaviours are coming from a place of abundance – where your self-worth is in a good place, where you know you are a kind and decent person whether or not you do this thing – or whether they're coming from a place of lack – where you need to please this person in order to feel better about yourself and feel worthy, accepted and approved of.

Truth #7
Someone else's success does not take from yours

Mark my words. If you manage to get to a point in life where you've successfully turned the volume down on your inner critic, the voice of self-doubt or imposter syndrome that resides within so many of us, or you manage to convince it that, despite what it whispers to you, you're not totally shit, it will be one of the greatest achievements of your life.

When you get to the final truth – truth #10 – you'll learn that I don't like to be particularly goal-oriented; that being said, truth #7 is one worth striving for.

I'm what you might call an over-sharer, someone with no filter, like, whatsoever. I once told an entire audience, among which included my mother and my elderly relatives, about the time my mother checked in with me about a previous relationship to make sure I was on the receiving end of an acceptable number of orgasms. I'm pretty sure I gave my seventy-something-year-old uncle a mild stroke, while my mother's face turned an irrevocable shade of puce. Your mother having a better sex life than you? Great! However, I don't tend to shout about this particular insecurity from the rooftops and the reason is because I'm afraid of how it makes me sound. On first impression, it's not the most endearing of anxieties to share.

Vocalising your feeling that someone's success has made you feel bad about yourself could ostensibly suggest that you just don't want other people to enjoy success. That you can't be happy for others when good things happen for them. Or worse, that you're the kind of person who needs to bring other people down to feel better about yourself or that you're just selfish and childish and jealous or even mean – and nobody wants to be that person.

Let's start by clearing that up. First of all, all of our insecurities are selfish in nature because they relate to the self. That's why we tend to keep them to ourselves. Secondly, describing them as childish is also fair, you might argue, because the part of our brain governing these threatening feelings – the amygdala – behaves like a child. And, yes, you are indeed experiencing jealousy and envy, but it's a perfectly natural human emotion. As long as you recognise it and address it, knowing that it's ultimately your issue and not theirs, it doesn't have to get ugly.

It's something you can manage and learn to flip it on its head. It only becomes mean if you act on it.

Social comparison

If you're feeling sensitive towards or even resentful of the success of those around you and you feel ashamed about these feelings, rest assured that it's an incredibly common, if rarely discussed, affliction. Nobody wants to admit that their green-eyed monster has struck again and, as such, we don't hear about it and we continue believing we're the only person feeling this way and if we really feel this way then what kind of person are we at all?

Though it can sound nasty on the surface, when you peel back the layers you'll see that it's not necessarily about wishing other people ill or wanting bad things to happen to them. And it's not that you can't be happy for others. You are not evil (well, I mean you could well be but I'm going to give you the benefit of the doubt here). What's more likely than all of these things is that the insecure part of your mind is taking another person's outward expression of achievement and using it as a mirror through which you evaluate yourself internally. It's known as social comparison. We all do it, we always have done and, yes, it's a real bitch.

Social comparison is a subject with which I've long been fasci-nated and have written about extensively. It seems to be so widely experienced and it impacts us in ways that appear to only be negative, yet it's one behaviour we really struggle to get a handle on.

With social comparison, you measure your own success and even your own self-worth against the success of others. Jealousy or envy can be a symptom of social comparison when you're stacking yourself against someone whom you view as similar to yourself, such as a colleague, a friend or someone whose achievements could be within the realm of possibility for you.

We don't tend to get caught up in the crosshairs of social comparison when it comes to someone we don't view ourselves as similar to. For example, I don't feel envious of my older brother's success as a financial whizzkid, because it's not something I can relate to or am interested in (in fact, if you asked me to perform a simple sum on the spot, I'm pretty sure I'd break out in hives). It's really only an issue I experience when someone has done something that I want to do or have tried to do. Someone whom I consider as part of my peer group, with similar ambitions to me.

With social comparison, how you view yourself privately, in your own head and behind the scenes, feels at odds with how successful you are perceiving your peers or those within your wheelhouse to be, and, of course, that could be professional success, social success – however you choose to define it.

Is there a difference between jealousy and envy?
Yep. While, conversationally, we will bounce between the words 'jealous' and 'envy' when describing the not so nice feelings I've chronicled in this chapter, there is technically a difference.

Envy is typically defined as the emotion of wanting what someone else has. You lack a desired attribute that someone else enjoys.

Jealousy, on the other hand, is an emotion under the fear umbrella, where we fear that something we possess or own will be taken from us.

Take the very common feelings of jealousy and envy when it comes to matters of the heart. If you want to be with someone who's already in a relationship with someone else, the emotion you might feel would be that of envy. You want what they have.

If you're the person in the relationship, however, and a third party makes a pass at your partner, the emotion you might feel would be jealousy. But, of course, you can sometimes feel both at the same time. You can be jealous that someone is flirting with your partner, fearing you could lose them, but you can also be envious that the person with whom your partner is flirting possesses attributes that you feel you lack, such as thinking they are better-looking than you.

Similarly, they might both be at play when it comes to social comparison and fearing that someone else's success would take from yours. You want what they have and you feel inferior in light of their success – the hallmarks of envy – but you are also afraid that your chance of success will be limited, or taken away from you, which we now understand as jealousy.

If you're trying to understand which emotion you're feeling – neither of which are any fun – you need to take the wider context into account.

Two kinds of envy

With passive social comparison, the feeling is almost always a case of envy, so let's stick with that for now.

The negative envy that we feel as a result of social comparison can manifest in one of two ways, according to Dr Robert L Leahy, author of *The Jealousy Cure*. There's what he calls 'depressive envy' and 'hostile envy' and we can experience them individually or both at the same time.

See if you can recognise either of them in yourself.

The former is what we feel when we take someone else's success and correlate it with our own perceived misfortune. For example, a peer does well and it makes you feel as though you're not good enough. You feel inferior. You feel down. You feel like a pile of pants. Sound familiar?

The latter is what you experience when you feel resentful about someone else's success (I'll take one for the team and raise my hand on this one too). Though, objectively, it's merely shining a light on your own insecurity, when it comes to hostile envy you can't quite see the wood for the trees. What you are seeing, through your own subjective and insecure lens, is someone who maybe doesn't deserve the success they've had. You might think someone just 'got lucky' or you'll find some other reason to minimise their success in your own mind in a bid to prevent yourself from feeling inferior. You might even do so in a bid to make yourself feel superior. Whichever type of envy you experience, neither is particularly favourable, and they are mentally draining. They encourage a culture of negative one-upmanship, where someone – either you or the person with whom you're comparing yourself – will always come out on the bottom.

Though your apparent similarities to someone may have triggered your social-comparison behaviours and your subsequent feelings of envy, it's actually got nothing to do with the person in question or the success they're enjoying at all. That's all irrelevant and you'll know this to be true if you've ever observed your thoughts during one stint of scrolling on Instagram: you'll find yourself comparing yourself with countless people. (Though I'm active on social media, I really do believe it has amplified our experience of social comparison to the nth degree.)

I believe it's about the meaning you have chosen to glean from the other person's success. It's how you make sense of it. It's what this success says to you about you, and where you're currently at – that's what it is for me – and whatever conclusions you arrive at, you can pretty much guarantee they're going to be skewed and entirely unreliable.

Meet Meredith

My own social-comparison monster has been known to bubble up on occasion, and when it does, it seems to yo-yo haphazardly between hostile and depressive envy. To be honest, it's reared its head so many times in my adult life that I should probably give it a name from here on out. Let's go with Meredith (named after chief antagonist Meredith Blake in the Lindsay Lohan movie *The Parent Trap*, obviously).

When Meredith strikes, I'll pick up the phone and relay her bitter message to my friend Jo (as she's someone I really don't mind showing the ugliest parts of myself to; we should all have someone like this in our lives). To give you an example: 'Am I a bad person because I saw so-and-so post about X and it made me feel both resentful and bad about myself?'

I cringe just typing this, but let me tell you about the knee-jerk feeling of toxic envy I've had in the past when someone I knew posted on social media about an anxiety book that, they said, 'changed their lives'. A book that everyone should read. A book that wasn't mine (my first book, *Owning It*, is all about anxiety and, to my own detriment, I look upon it as a first-born child).

Knowing Meredith better than I do, Jo got straight to work, helping me to box her in before she could wreak too much havoc. Jo said, 'No, you're not a horrible person for feeling this way. First of all, we all have a Meredith inside of us, most of us just keep her a secret, whereas you vocalise everything. Second of all, you think you're having ill feelings towards that person and their book, but what you're actually having are ill feelings towards yourself, which is no good thing either. Their success is making you feel bad, not about them but about you.'

OK, that makes sense. But why does it make me feel bad about myself? When I took a moment to unpack this ugly and automatic response further, I could admit that, yes, I did feel threatened and insecure. I felt jealous and envious all at once. And because I felt threatened, my response was a self-defensive desire for this poor person's book to fail. If someone else had told me that this book was actually crap, and that I needn't worry, I'd have honestly felt better (and, yes, I'm still feeling like one mighty arsehole for committing this to print).

Jo was right, though, it had nothing to do with the book or the person who wrote it. It could have been anybody and any book. It was affecting me because I felt that success in this particular area was somehow finite and that if this other book was doing well, it would mean that mine would suffer (jealousy) and I wanted the success they were currently enjoying (envy). *There's only so much room for books about anxiety*, I thought, as if there's only one success pie in the world and that we're all clamouring, elbows out, for our piece. I felt that it would take from me, that it would set me back and mean my book wouldn't have its fair chance to flourish. I even felt that if this book was so apparently good, it had to mean that mine, by comparison, was not. Ridiculous as it sounds on paper, thanks to a cocktail of social comparison, jealousy and envy, complete with a dash of imposter syndrome, this was what I truly believed.

On top of this, I also had to acknowledge that, despite my best efforts in recent years, I was still slipping into old habits of attaching my feelings of worthiness and of being good enough to external factors such as professional success, which is something that's always going to fluctuate and be outside of my control.

In Chapter 6, we spoke about the external validation mental model and how so many of us unknowingly rely on it as a way to measure our self-worth. It's OK to want the validation of the people you care about. That will be important to you. It's also OK to care a lot about your professional endeavours. But when it comes to your self-worth, these should not be determining factors. We need to remind ourselves once in a while to derive our self-worth from internal factors, which are things that we can control ourselves.

More helpful measures of our self-worth include:

o how we treat other people
o living with integrity and self-respect
o honouring our core values
o working to the best of our ability at whatever we take on
o our personal satisfaction at life
o the quality of our relationships.

Of all the truths laid bare in this book, this truth – that another person's success does not take from mine – has been the one that I've found most difficult to embrace. Let's say it again but this time we'll pause for dramatic effect ... Another person's success does not take from yours.

Sounds simple, right? Sounds obvious, even. Well sure, if you're a perfectly well-adjusted, fully functioning human, but I can't claim to know too many of them. The thing is, while I write these words and know that it makes sense in my rational mind, really believing it for myself (or more specifically, getting my inner oppressor to believe it) is no easy task. Why is that? The answer is that I have a zero-sum game mentality.

A zero-sum game mentality

When I really began to cross-examine these negative feelings and behaviours, I realised that it all comes down to one specific thing. One belief. The reason I was experiencing all of these nasty feelings and grappling with these unhelpful thoughts – and why you might be too – is because I was perceiving the world as a zero-sum game – in other words: 'If she or he wins, I lose.'

And if we decide that someone winning or having success means we're losing out, then jealousy or envy, and all of those nasty social-comparison side-effects, will surely rise to the fore. Again, don't feel bad about this, it's very normal and it's so easy to slip into. As Dr Leahy further explains, when we operate with a zero-sum game mentality, we'll have a hard time not being the 'winner'.

Typically, this is a mentality we experience as children when playing games, but it can absolutely spill over into our adult lives too if we're not aware of it. And much like kids in a playground, Leahy explains, we often feel better about ourselves if we (you and the person with whom you're comparing yourself) both lose (whatever your perception of losing or failing is) than if one loses and the other wins.

Why do we subscribe to zero-sum game beliefs?

Yes, I'm going to pull the evolution card again. Here we have yet another thing that we experience in our contemporary lives that we can trace right back to our earliest times.

The more I thought about the zero-sum game mentality, the more I correlated it with a fear of scarcity: we fear that opportunities are limited. We are motivated to pursue things, and essentially to win, based on this fear. This was useful back in hunter-gatherer times when opportunities for food and shelter (the very things we depended on for our survival) were quite literally scarce. The struggle was real. We needed to act on opportunities that presented themselves to us because if we failed to seize them, our survival would be in question.

This might also explain why we became competitive in the first place. Someone else's success could well mean our misfortune or vice versa. The fear of scarcity was valid back then and it's been relevant throughout history during times of famine or war, but today it's less of an issue. Though our survival is not necessarily in question – when it comes to professional or romantic success, for example – the primitive part of our brain still reacts as though it is (in fact, survival is really all your brain cares about) and then envy pops up. We might not be aware of it or identify it as a fear we experience, but it's likely at play in your subconscious, thanks to our evolutionary conditioning.

Instinctively, we apply the same fear of scarcity and the same 'survival of the fittest' logic to modern-day opportunities. We want what others have because we need resources to survive, not just comforts in order to thrive.

Is there a solution?
Solutions to the scourge of social comparison have been well explored in behavioural psychology, but beyond telling yourself that you're on your own 'journey' – thanks Pinterest, problem solved – or stopping yourself from scrolling your social media feed, which isn't always feasible, not a lot has really stuck.

Sure, we can physically remove the temptation to compare by limiting our social media usage. And I must say that the mute button on Instagram has been a huge help for me – out of sight, out of mind – but these techniques are slapping a temporary plaster on your social-comparison tendencies, and they're not helping prevent it in the first place, so we need to dig a little deeper.

One thing I'm a big advocate of is temporal comparison. It's a great alternative to social comparison and it's one that I've delved into in previous books. It's where we swap our comparison with others for comparison with ourselves alone. You take yourself of today and compare it to yourself of the past or you imagine yourself in the future. This keeps things relative to you and your circumstances alone. You become your own yardstick, putting the blinkers on when it comes to everybody else and instead honing in on where you are, where you've been and where you want to be (figuratively speaking). You bring your attention to the only thing you can safely rely on: your own progress, which you then detach from everyone else.

What I've since realised, however, is that for temporal comparison to really work and become more than just a nice idea, we have to ask ourselves why we struggle with this in the first place. The answer, I would offer, lies in the self-excavation of your feelings, behaviours and beliefs. By identifying whether or not you're living your life through a zero-sum game lens, and then – and this is the clincher – the conscious dismantling of this incredibly unhelpful belief that is, in my opinion, at the core of all unhealthy social comparison.

Only then can we really accept and believe the truth that someone else's success doesn't take from ours.

How to challenge your zero-sum game mentality
So now we understand why the zero-sum game mentality is an issue. This is good. It means we have something tangible on which to focus, where positive change might occur and make our lives a little bit easier.

In order to stop operating within this debilitating mindset, my first port of call would be my old reliable friend, Cognitive

Behavioural Therapy (CBT). As we know from the truth about change (Chapter 2), it's something we need to carve out time for, to work on consistently, as this way of thinking has become our brain's well-trodden path. With CBT, you bring your attention to the thoughts, feelings and behaviours that keep you stuck in this particular worldview. Writing a journal is particularly helpful as a practical way to begin tracking your automatic thoughts and how they make you feel.

As we've explored, the thoughts might revolve around 'this person has got this amazing new job and I am unsuccessful compared to her'. You may feel sadness, anxiety, anger, jealousy, envy (and then shame about the envy) and discouragement. The behaviour as a result of these thoughts and feelings might be to give up on something you're working on. To withdraw yourself from your efforts because they seem futile when compared to this other person.

Or it could be to say something mean about the other person. Ask yourself (in your journal) what your thoughts and feelings are the next time you feel that someone else's success takes from yours - it might not be so obvious as to ruin your day but it could be a little negative niggle while scrolling social media. Then ask yourself how you acted on these thoughts and feelings. And do this without judgement. You can write these down privately as opposed to printing them in a book for all the world to see (points finger at self). Just observe where your thoughts are at, what narrative they're feeding you. This is your starting point and should come easy to you.

When that part's done, gently, it's time to switch tactic and (as my editor so eloquently once said of my perpetual self-doubt) bulldoze right through it.

This is the part of *The Parent Trap* when they get their own back on Meredith and send her packing, on an air mattress, into the middle of a lake. (She really was the ultimate 1990s villain and this revenge was absolutely deserved and if you haven't watched it you really should but worry not, this is as far as my referencing of this movie goes.) So – are these thoughts accurate? Do they have any basis in reality? Be tough on your thoughts here – they're distorted, though you might not yet believe it, and they're doing you no favours.

Write down a more measured, reasonable alternative to your original thoughts. Lead with fact, not opinion. For example: 'This person has got this amazing new job. This does not change anything about where I'm at or what I'm doing.' The all-or-nothing thoughts, having been so automatic for so long, will keep coming, but you don't have to opt in to them. You can choose to decide that, while you hear them, you no longer have to believe them.

Remember, it's a narrative your mind is feeding you; it's not necessarily the truth. Ultimately, by doing this, you're working towards dismantling your existing belief that someone else's success takes from yours and replacing it with the truth that says someone else's success does *not* take from yours.

Below is an example of a CBT thought-recording exercise to challenge zero-sum game beliefs.

EVENT   →   **What happened?**

For example: 'I saw somebody post about getting their dream job on Instagram.'

....

AUTOMATIC →   **What went on in your head as**
THOUGHT   **you received this information?**

For example: 'I'll never get my dream job.'
'I don't have any good news to post.'
'There's not enough success to go around and she's getting all of it.'

....

FEELING   →   **How did these thoughts make you feel?**

For example: 'Frustrated, discouraged, self-critical, sad, envious, resentful.'

....

BEHAVIOUR →   **Did you act on them? What did you do?**

For example: 'I tried to think of ways I might be as good as or better than this person.'

'I put them down to make myself feel better.'

'I got distracted from my own work and got nothing done.'

DISPUTE	→ **Look at the facts; are these thoughts based on facts or just your opinion?**
	For example: 'Do I even want that job for myself?' 'No.'
	'Does this person's success have any bearing on my own?' 'No.'
	'Am I affected in any way other than social comparison here?' 'No.'

....

MORE REASONABLE THOUGHT	→ **What would be a more helpful alternative that's more likely to be true?**
	For example: 'I can be happy for her.'
	'This has nothing to do with me.'
	'I am doing my own thing and should take this as motivation to keep going.'

Why someone else's success doesn't take from yours

Granted, there may well be times in life when you're up against someone else for a promotion, and, if they get, it will feel very literally that because they've been successful, you are not. But, even in this scenario, as shit as it feels, it's not true. You've lost out on that one opportunity but you are not cut off from all others when you step back and look at your career as a whole. A co-worker getting a promotion today does not mean you won't get as good a job in the near future or one that's actually better suited to you.

Outside of scenarios where you are pitted against someone, if you're looking at things objectively, you will struggle to find evidence that supports the idea that someone else's success can actually take from yours.

Your friend who has more money than you is not taking money from you. They're not getting in the way of your earning potential.

The book that reaches number one on the bestseller list. There isn't just one number one for all of time. It doesn't stop people from enjoying your book. It doesn't mean yours also can't do well.

The person with thousands of followers is not blocking you from building your own following, if that's what's important to you.

When you take a step back, which I like to call the helicopter approach, where you've got a much better view of things, there are very few things in life that have a limited supply. Another person's success has absolutely nothing to do with you and the sense of scarcity for success you feel is a fabrication of your insecurity.

Healthy envy

You can bring this truth – that another person's success is not related to yours – into your awareness every day, and that alone will be a huge help. It, along with a regular temporal-comparison practice and CBT, will certainly stop your feelings from escalating, but we can't realistically expect ourselves to never feel envious or jealous. That's like pressuring ourselves to never feel anxious or stressed, which is a sure-fire way to feel both of those things. Instead, we sometimes need to accept envy as a natural human emotion and then make it work for us.

If you've been with me since *Owning It* was published, you will know that I'm not about curing things or making things go away, but rather, turning them around to become something useful. We've already covered the two kinds of envy defined by Dr Robert L Leahy - depressive and hostile - but there is a third kind of envy that's a little more useful: benign envy.

Depressive and hostile envy are maladaptive - they do us harm, they make us feel bad. But benign envy, which is more adaptive, still allows for it without having it negatively impact you. Benign envy is what we experience when we acknowledge somebody's success and we are impressed by it and encouraged to take action. We might still look to others as a representation of where we would like to be, but we don't use their success as a tool to beat ourselves up with. We use it as a tool to inspire us.

We are always naturally going to have our attention drawn towards other people's success, especially if it's within the same realm as that which we are striving for, but with benign envy, we can choose to learn something from it and foster what's often referred to in popular psychology as a 'growth mindset'.

Do you have a growth mindset or a fixed mindset?
Coined by Professor Carol Dweck of Stanford University, a growth mindset is one where you believe that you are always evolving and learning and improving, where you might

sometimes take two steps back but then you'll take one step forward. It's where you exert effort to move forward and you persist in the face of perceived setbacks. Conversely, a fixed mindset is where we believe that we are born and raised with a fixed set of skills and abilities that will determine how far we'll go and the level of success we can enjoy. With a fixed mindset, we might hit a roadblock and then get stuck. Not ideal but certainly something you could change, in the same way we've already challenged your zero-sum game belief.

When you develop your own growth mindset, you can take the envy that you're sure to feel from time to time and then use it as a resource. Instead of 'I'm a loser because they're successful', we can take note of what they've done and apply it to ourselves – 'I'm impressed by her tenacity, I'm going to keep pushing through my own self-doubt.'

You'll notice your growth mindset is growing and working for you when you no longer get stopped in your tracks by social comparison. Without it, you'd get stuck, you'd feel discouraged, but with it, you can consciously choose benign envy, rather than falling victim to its negative counterparts.

Developing your own growth mindset
To develop your own growth mindset, you will need to start with ... can you guess? Yes, gold star for you – you will need to start with a willingness to be vulnerable. Why? Because, among other things, with a growth mindset you have to take steps towards challenges and opportunities where there are risks

involved, where you might make mistakes or fail and you have to believe that if things don't go your way, you haven't actually lost, you've grown.

You need to change the narrative that sees these moments in life as challenges and instead recognise them as opportunities. You also need to view yourself as a constant work in progress. You will not progress every day – and we definitely need days to just be – but, overall, you're trending in the direction of where you want to be. You need to be realistic with yourself and patient, knowing that things take time. You need to watch your thoughts and how you speak to yourself, how you react in the face of social comparison and choose the benign end of the envy spectrum.

When your growth mindset starts to take shape, your zero-sum game belief will start to dissolve. Throughout this book, though I'm only now bringing it to your attention, we have been working on cultivating a healthy growth mindset.

I asked Dr Tchiki Davis, author of *Click Here for Happiness* and founder of the Berkeley Well-being Institute (or in short, very impressive woman), for her two cents on the growth mindset, as it's something she's explored extensively in her work.

To be living with a growth mindset, she says, 'We have to view living as learning. When we do, we start to pursue scary things, try new things, and make an effort to learn from our mistakes.' It's important because if you want to make a change in your life, 'you need to believe you can change, and if you actually believe that change is possible, you're more likely to put in the effort that it takes to change'.

On top of a willingness to be vulnerable and the points I've raised thus far, Davis also suggests it's good to have a pretty clear idea of how a growth mindset and a fixed mindset differ, so that you can identify which one you're in. You might, at times, slip into a fixed mindset (I certainly do, and it's easy for that to happen when we are stressed out or exhausted) but with awareness you can nudge yourself back in the growth direction. Davis cites three key differences to be mindful of:

1. Effort

When faced with hard work, the 'fixed mindset' person may recruit others to do the hardest parts, spending as little effort as possible, while the 'growth mindset' person believes that good outcomes often require exertion – 'effort' is just a part of the process. In order to master a new task, one usually needs to apply energy, whether mental, physical or simply by using repetition over time.

2. Challenge

A 'fixed mindset' person shies away from challenges, possibly from fear of failure and may go into hiding as a way to avoid responsibilities. In contrast, the 'growth mindset' person finds challenges to be exciting and engaging, knowing that they will learn something valuable from their experiences. They 'stick to it,' mastering the challenge, and then are able to move on to ever greater accomplishments.

3. Mistakes and Feedback

The 'fixed mindset' person hates making mistakes because it's embarrassing. They may blame others or be defensive when criticised. Meanwhile, a 'growth mindset' person will see the mistake as a lesson to learn from and will be less likely to take criticism personally. Being open to criticism can help improve one's ability to do better the next time, which is another reason why a 'growth mindset' can lead to success.

 PAUSE FOR THOUGHT

As this chapter concludes, I know what needs to happen in order to accept the truth that someone else's success doesn't take from mine, but I also acknowledge that this kind of change won't happen overnight. My thoughts are used to jumping to their well-learned, negative conclusions.

What I have now though is a set of tools that will help me the next time I find myself stuck in a social-comparison spiral. Should another book about anxiety hit the **New York Times** *bestseller list, which it will, I will take a moment to see where my envy or jealousy is really coming from. Is it that I want to be on that bestseller list? (Yes, yes it is, but all in good time.) Is it that I'm linking this kind of success to my self-worth? If it is, I need to remind myself of healthier ways to measure my self-worth.*

I can challenge my thoughts with what I know to be fact, using CBT. I can go back to the zero-sum game mentality and make sure it's not in the driving seat. I can practise temporal comparison by looking at how far I've come. I can allow myself to feel envy but choose benign envy instead. With benign envy I can look at another person's success and ask myself: 'What can I do that's different? Is there a way to set myself apart? What worked for this person and what can I learn from them? What did they get right?' I can flip the envy on its head and turn it into a very useful resource.

I can do any and all of these things, knowing all the while that I'm laying the unwavering foundations of my own growth mindset which can only be a good thing. And if all else fails, there's always the mute button.

Below is a toolkit for social comparison:

- *Do a CBT thought record exercise in your journal.*
- *Ask yourself where jealousy is coming from.*
- *Check in with how you measure your self-worth and shift it towards things you can control.*
- *Practise temporal comparison using a journal.*
- *Choose benign envy.*
- *Reframe another person's success as motivation for you.*
- *Bring your attention back to growth mindset.*
- *Curate your social media feed so as to ensure it's only showing you content that makes you feel at ease about yourself.*

CHAPTER 8

Truth #8
If you want to be happy, you're doing it wrong

In all the self-help seminars and well-being books that exist in the world, there's one question they're all striving to answer: How can you be happy?

Now clearly, from the other chapters in this book, and the truths with which I've struggled, there's very little I can claim to know or have yet figured out (well, you'd hope I'd at least figured a few things out by the time I sent this book to print). Happiness, though, is something I'm pretty good at. Big claim, I know, but by and large, I really am a very happy person. In this chapter, I'm going to dive deep into some of the essential ingredients which, in my experience, come together with a lot of what we've already covered to enable this most coveted way of being.

Before I get to that part, however, there's something we need to do. We've got to take this word 'happiness' we speak of, put it in a box marked 'unrealistic' and push it to one side. We need to swap out happiness for contentment.

Really, when we talk about wanting to achieve happiness in our day-to-day lives, we're talking about wanting to achieve contentment. So, allow me to say what I actually mean: contentment is something I am good at. I am generally a very contented – if a little bit neurotic – person.

As far as I'm concerned, feeling content for the most part, while allowing for days when you're bound to feel crappy or just so-so, is a high enough aim. Striving for happiness is where we're going wrong, hence the truth that is this chapter.

We can define contentment as the feeling of satisfaction with life. Contentment is understood to be deeper and longer-lasting while happiness, on which we're all a bit misguided, is far more fleeting. Happiness is linked with heightened moments of joy and, yes, more of those would be nice, but to feel this way every day is just unsustainable. We're chasing it only to find that what we're really chasing is our tails. We can all experience happiness spikes when good things happen in our lives – for example, the birth of a child, achieving something we've been working hard towards, even a day spent shopping – but when the initial flood of excitement, and the happy hormones that go along with it, subsides we will always settle back down to some kind of neurological resting point. This is true of people who scoop the lottery jackpot or get a promotion.

It's also true in reverse, when bad things happen to us: pretty soon, we'll find that same baseline again. You'll recognise this in yourself when something doesn't go your way. You're usually over it by the following week; it no longer impacts your mood with the same intensity that you first felt.

Known as hedonistic adaptation, this is why someone in the developing world, living on less than you or I could ever fathom, is able to feel just as content as those of us who enjoy great privilege – we all return to our relative baseline. And I believe it's precisely this baseline that we need to hone in on, and do what we can to ensure it's sitting comfortably within the contentment bracket.

This, I would argue, is a far more worthwhile place to be. Much less intimidating than the pursuit of those lofty happiness spikes, contentment is something that everyone can achieve and, more importantly, it's something we can sustain.

When we start focusing our attention on this baseline, you'll notice something bigger starts to happen: we rethink the old maxim of 'I'll be happy when ...' or 'I'll be happy if ...' – something that seems to drive a lot of us, no matter how much we're told it's an illusion. Instead, we move towards the idea that contentment is something we can start to develop right here, right now. With this logic, it's not so much about finding more opportunities for isolated spikes of happiness, but more about fortifying our everyday baseline. Instead of living most of our lives at an unsatisfactory baseline and seeking out those temporary peaks, we train our focus on the resting point and do what we can to gently raise that up. Make sense?

What's more, if we take this idea a little bit further (while, of course, allowing for the fact that this is merely a theory of mine and not based on anything concrete), I would also suggest that in raising your everyday baseline, you might also strengthen your resilience.

What I mean by this is that by elevating your resting point a few notches, which means it will then sit higher than it did before, when you next experience a setback (the plunging alternative to the happiness peak) you'll be experiencing it from a higher point, and therefore it might not dip quite as far down as it used to. You won't be affected by pitfalls to the same extent that you may have been before when your default setting was lower, and, as an added bonus, you'll probably find that you bounce back more easily. That's resilience.

What's more, when you begin to add things to your life that raise your level of contentment, then you can fall back on these when things get tougher - you create a contentment cushion for yourself.

Now that we know what we're dealing with, here's the big question: what exactly is it that contributes towards a more contented baseline?

If you're looking for one simple answer, it's this (and unfortunately it's not all that simple): contentment, and well-being generally, is what happens when our bio-psycho-social markers sit in harmony, merging beautifully at the centre of the Venn diagram that is our individual experience of life.

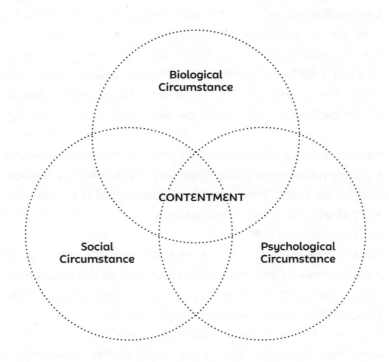

Let me explain this a little further.

There are three key elements we can look towards that help determine our well-being:

1 our biological circumstance – how you were made, any biological predispositions you have
2 our social circumstance – in other words our environment, our relationships, our lifestyle
3 our psychological circumstance – our beliefs and attitudes, our coping skills, etc.

All of these three elements overlap and influence each other (hence the delightfully hyperbolic term I invite you to bust out at your next dinner party, 'biopsychosocial').

For sure, your socio-economic circumstances will have an awful lot to do with how content you're going to be. If you have food and shelter, if you have enough money to get by, etc. all of this will significantly impact your baseline. But beyond these basic needs, countless studies have shown that having ten times more money or twenty times more followers on social media doesn't seem to make us any more content in the long term.

Your unique biology is also said to play a big role in how content you're going to be in life; for example, some brains are naturally more predisposed to depression or anxiety, just as some brains will find it easier to relax or react to stimuli in more helpful ways. But these elements of biology and sociology don't stand alone, nor are they set in stone, impermeable to change.

Your biology will be influenced by your environment and your experience of your environment will be influenced by your biology. For example, you could start with the ideal neurological conditions for a contented mind but then have them hampered by a toxic environment. Or you could be in a very good social environment with a great job and great friends which serve, over time, to create a more contented neurological picture, even though you might have started out at a biological disadvantage. But there's a third element we often overlook: the psychological. Your attitude and your outlook and how you look after yourself from a psychological perspective will also have an effect on your experience of your environment as well as your biology, and vice versa. (Look back to the Venn diagram if your head is starting to hurt!)

It's here, within this psychological space, that I believe we have the most power to affect change. It's here that we, as individuals, have the most control, and it's here that this book has been focused.

If we go back once more to the idea of the very contented person who lives in what you might consider an unfavourable environment in a developing nation, we can posit that it's their psychological circumstances (their positive attitude, their gratitude for what they do have as opposed to their focus on what they do not have, etc.) that they're getting right, which then positively impacts the other two elements, raising their contentment baseline. All three elements are equally important, they're all interlinked, but where one is struggling, another may step in to pick up the slack.

For the purposes of this chapter, I'm going to assume you have your basic needs of food and shelter met, and that you're relatively healthy in the physical sense so that we can hone right in on some specific psychological tools that will serve to strengthen our contentment baseline every day. These ingredients, as well as what we've already explored throughout this book, have certainly proven to be invaluable for me when it comes to maintaining my goal of keeping my contentment boat afloat.

They are as follows:

1. Vulnerability

'Vulnerability again? Christ, we get it,' I hear you say. Well, of course I'm going to suggest that a willingness to be vulnerable tops this list. Why? Because when we allow ourselves to be vulnerable and authentic, we stop creating tension by trying to be something we're not, and, thus, we feel more at ease.

Our internal friction settles down (soothing the bio in 'biopsychosocial'). We become more accepting of ourselves and we remove the pressure of having to appear (to ourselves or to the world) to have everything figured out right at this moment. We accept that we are a work in progress (remember your growth mindset?) and that we have our limitations, and we become more content with ourselves as a result.

That's one reason.

The reason I return to vulnerability again in this context, however, is that, with it, we open ourselves up to the possibility of more meaningful connections with other human beings: the very thing our social species' well-being thrives on, which, in turn, helps to satisfy the social in 'biopsychosocial'.

With vulnerability, we become more compassionate towards others, we relate to people better and they do the same with us. It takes us beyond the superficial level of acquaintance, forging a more authentic and lasting bond. It's precisely this meaningful connection – for which vulnerability is an obvious prerequisite – that has been found time and time again to play a most significant role in contributing towards our feelings of long-term contentment and satisfaction.

But here's the thing – it's not about having an impressive social network. Emphasis on the word 'meaningful' is key here.

Sure, you can certainly connect with countless people at a surface (or even digital) level, but only when two people get to their most authentic selves can it be the kind of relationship that makes you feel good. For lasting contentment, we need to look beyond quantity and instead seek out quality relationships where there is social support. And for that social-support element, we need vulnerability. It doesn't mean we have to be vulnerable with the whole world, and we don't need to gather enough friends to build an army – it need only be as few as two people to whom you are not afraid to show your true self, where there is an intrinsic sense of support, that goes both ways and beyond Instagram DMs.

Whether we consider ourselves introverts or extroverts, it doesn't really matter. This need for social connection is common to every single one of us, as is the fact that we are all vulnerable in some way. And so, we need to lean into this nature, focusing on our most valued relationships wherever there is room for them, rather than filling our time exclusively with individual, non-social, personal goal-oriented activities. The thing is, we don't just feel better with social connection and social support, our baseline of contentment depends on it.

To illustrate the significance of social connection when it comes to my own contentment, I'm going to pull out another of my miniature violins for a trip down memory lane. Indulge me if you will.

So, I used to feel bad about the fact that I don't have one solid group of best friends with whom I've hung out since I was in nappies. Where a lot of people make their social connections very early on in life and stick with them right through to adulthood, it really wasn't until I was in my twenties that I made the connections that contribute most to my current sense of contentment. More specifically, it wasn't until I was willing to embrace my own vulnerability that I was able to develop the kinds of relationships that mean the most to me today.

Being in my thirties now, I know that quality beats quantity any day, but there was a time when I was quite honestly embarrassed by my lack of a 'squad', particularly as I made the transition from secondary school (late teens) to university (early twenties). I was by no means a social pariah, but towards my latter school days I did go through a very hard time with anxiety and stomach issues. The very age when you're supposed to be gaining and asserting your independence.

While my peers were more interested in getting as far away from their comfort zones as possible, spending more and more time socialising and getting excited about their college adventures and what adult life would have in store, I was the complete and total opposite. I shut myself off from pretty much all social activities, choosing instead to stay at home, distracting myself with my monstrous DVD collection and the company of my parents and dog, because I felt safer there and because at home I wouldn't have to pretend to be something I was not (also, let's be honest: with horrendous stomach issues you just kinda want the comfort of your own bathroom too).

I was so closed in by my anxiety, I even chose my degree and the college where I would obtain it based on proximity to my house (about a ten-minute walk). When open days popped up for other colleges in the same city (let alone in other cities), I made up excuse after excuse as to why I couldn't go check them out. Really, I was just too scared to consider studying anywhere that took me away from my literal comfort zone. I may as well have been attached to my home and my parents by a piece of string. I never ventured far enough for it to break.

Because of my age, my lack of understanding and a general dearth of awareness surrounding anxiety at the time, I was afraid to articulate how I was really feeling to anybody that I deemed a close friend.

'What's wrong with you?' they would ask. 'Are you still sick?'

'Yeah I'm not really sure, it must be some freak bug.'

I felt stupid and embarrassed and like the only person my age who felt this way, so, naturally, I didn't dare talk about it. Why couldn't I just go to the party and have fun like everyone else? Why was I stuck in the bathroom where said party was happening, having a panic attack because just being there was too much for me, and phoning my mother in the hope that she would come pick me up?

While the anxiety and the stomach issues obviously hoovered up a huge portion of my contentment at that age, the withdrawal from social connections (the missed class trips, the parties I'd only hear about through the grapevine, the lack of live-in-each-other's-pockets closeness that's typical of this age group), born out of a fear of revealing my vulnerability, really took its toll on me. I left school with plenty of acquaintances, but not one person with whom I felt really connected or remained close to the present day.

Poor me! But I'll put my tiny violin back in its box now because eventually, things got better.

Even though I did only venture as far as ten minutes from my house to further my education (I don't know how I would have coped if I lived in rural Ireland), it was there that I found my tribe, the people with whom I could eventually be myself and depend upon for social support (and fun and adventure and all of that other important stuff that we get from our relationships).

These days, I have the same handful of very close friends (not necessarily one big group but pockets of gems here and there) whom I credit heavily with keeping my baseline in excellent shape. They've been there, every step of the way as I eventually pieced myself back together.

That's not to say the friends I had in school weren't up to the task – not at all. It's that I never allowed myself to be vulnerable enough to let them in. I didn't give anybody the chance because I was afraid of what people would think of me. I denied myself of the relationships I needed in order to feel content. Sometimes, these days, I'll think that by spending more time alone, I'm practising self-care. I'll start to fall into my hermit-like tendencies because, anxiety or not, I am definitely a home bird. But put me across a table from any one of my close friends today (and perhaps throw a bottle of Prosecco in between us), even when I feel my pyjamas calling, and I'll quickly remember how vital this social connection and support really is, enabled today by my unapologetic vulnerability.

My point?

Don't underestimate the influence that social connection can exert over your contentment baseline, and if you feel that you're lacking in that department, unleash the V! (that's V for vulnerability, not vagina, just in case).

So that's one crucial psychological ingredient covered. However, as important as social connection is for contentment, you will still need to allow for solo time, in order to benefit from the second psychological ingredient in my contentment recipe.

2. Flow

No, this is not just about 'going with the flow', although I'm sure that would definitely help to boost your contentment baseline too. The 'flow' I'm talking about here refers to what *Positive Psychology* describes as 'the positive mental state of being completely absorbed, focused and involved in an activity at a certain point in time, while also deriving enjoyment from being engaged in that activity'.

First popularised by psychologist Mihaly Csikszentmihalyi in 1975 (try saying that when you're three drinks deep), 'flow' is something we've probably all experienced, though we might not be aware when we're in it. It is one of the most wonderful, self-rewarding and contentment-boosting states of being there is and not a drop of alcohol is required. Finding your flow is not a case of passively enjoying a movie or getting lost in a juicy book; it's got to have the personal involvement and progress aspects too, as well as a little bit of enjoyment thrown in for good measure.

The perfect example of psychological flow that I've experienced is during those times when the writer's block with which

I'm often plagued starts to lift and I manage to bash out a few thousand words in one go, with no concept of how much time has passed and no awareness of anything else that's going on around me. Obviously, when that happens, it becomes an activity I thoroughly enjoy and feel immensely satisfied by. But it's not exclusive to unblocked authors.

I know Barry, my husband, gets it all the time as an electronic engineer, as he finds his own mental monkey blissfully lost down a coding ravine (which sure as hell wouldn't be flow-inducing for me). Hours could go by while he's deep in flow, oblivious to the outside world, along with my 'will you please stop at the shop on your way home and get me some chocolate?' texts. It might sound like a rare unicorn we should be so lucky to find but thankfully it's not. It's often where you least expect it. It's something I can even experience when I'm immersed in an Excel spreadsheet, believe it or not, getting on top of my expenses and my income tax. As dull as that might sound, after a while I become focused and engaged and if I'm not hitting any roadblocks, I will effortlessly enter the flow state of mind.

I also enjoy it because I know that doing it is a very good use of my time and it makes me feel more organised and then I have the benefit of longer-lasting satisfaction. I feel the same way sometimes when I'm rearranging my wardrobe and I've also noticed I can enter the flow state when I'm busy writing product press releases, which is one of the more unglamorous ways in which I pay the bills. I'm not exactly riveted by the activity on paper and it's hardly impressive work but my brain really likes the task while I'm doing it. It's challenging but I'm good at it. It's like giving a Rubik's cube to someone who, with a little bit of effort, is more than capable of solving it.

Similar in some ways to mindfulness and meditation, with flow you are rooted to the present moment, focused on nothing more than the here and now. What differentiates it though is your involvement and the presence of some kind of short-term goal, e.g. the goal to clean my wardrobe or write some copy, as well as the instant feedback of my progress.

What I find most inspiring about the concept of flow is that clearly, it's something we can enjoy when doing any kind of work or activity, even something that's typically deemed a menial task – take basic data entry, for example, which may or may not be your brain's jam.

As explained by Csikszentmihalyi, flow has nothing to do with ego. When you enter the flow state, he says, 'the ego falls away' and when this happens, we feel at ease and we're no longer concerned about perception. Because of this, we don't have to aim outrageously high to achieve flow. You can find it whether you're at intern level or CEO, whether you're in a professional context or at home. Whether you're painting the next master-piece or baking some Rice Krispie cakes. It doesn't have to be something super creative or cerebral and you do not have to be an artist to experience flow, though artists will definitely be familiar with the state of being. For an artist, psychological flow might well be the elusive unicorn they're hoping to stumble upon. For the rest of us, it serves as an essential and often underestimated tool for optimising our contentment baseline.

Following on from Csikszentmihalyi's seminal work on the subject back in the 1970s, research has continued to focus on the correlation between flow and increased productivity. This is why there's been so much interest in it, because if people can optimise their creativity and their performance, that will surely be good for business. What I'm more interested in, though, is how the experience of flow correlates with increased contentment.

For a start, we can look to neurocognitive professor Arne Dietrich whose research explores the neuroscience of flow and how it impacts the brain's function. In his 2004 paper, he explains that when we enter the flow state, we free ourselves of self-talk and self-analysis. Known as 'transient hypofrontality', flow sees a relaxing of the prefrontal cortex, which is normally involved in self-consciousness, self-talk and analytical thinking. In other words, when you enter the flow state, you turn off the (typically negative) voice inside your head. Your ego gets back in its box while the limbic regions of the brain happily engage in the task at hand. By entering the flow state, which enables transient hypofrontality, you're creating literal headspace where your brain's normally erratic activity calms right down into a nice, soothing rhythm. As I said in Chapter 7, anything that lowers the volume on our inner critic – or manages to switch it off entirely for a period of time, as is the case with flow – can only be a good thing for our sense of long-term well-being. With regular transient hypofrontality, we feel more relaxed, more creative and, yes, more content.

Beyond these functional shifts, flow also sees positive change in our brain's neurochemistry, by offering up a mixture of gorgeous, feel-good hormones and neurotransmitters. When you enter the flow state, your brain enjoys a release of dopamine, serotonin, noradrenalin, endorphins and anandamide all at once. Let's look at each one briefly.

Dopamine you'll already be familiar with as it's often referred to as the main feel-good hormone. We get a hit of dopamine as a reward when we have positive experiences, sometimes as a result of movement, but in this case it's a reward for our enjoyed focused attention.

Serotonin is another happiness hero. It's a mood stabiliser that regulates our emotions and plays a big role in controlling our sleep/wake cycle.

Noradrenalin is actually classified as a stress hormone because it's triggered by the sympathetic nervous system and produced when we experience fight or flight. In this case, it's not a negative stress but a more positive arousal that sharpens our senses and our ability to perform.

Endorphins, which are typically associated with exercise, are also triggered by the flow state. These are natural pain-blockers that reduce stress.

Lastly, anandamide is an endocannabinoid (something you might recognise if you're a fan of CBD) involved with mood regulation that also boasts anti-anxiety and anti-depressant properties.

With this cocktail of super sexy hormones engaged by flow, you experience a wonderful by-product: stress, worry, anxiety, and unhelpful and disruptive thoughts dissolve into the background and all that's left is contentment. So, you want more flow in your life? Great. First, you will need to adopt a mindset that favours what Csikszentmihalyi calls the 'autotelic experience' over the end result. Think of all those cheesy posts that tell you to enjoy the journey itself rather than the destination. The more Csikszentmihalyi teased apart the correlation between flow and happiness, the more he realised that what we typically associate with happiness – i.e. a life with lots of money where we don't have to do any work, where we can just watch Netflix and eat brunch every day – is the last place we're going to find it.

Contrary to popular belief, and something that I'm hoping will stop me from wasting any more money on lottery tickets, constant leisure is not the answer; idleness would only see our baseline nosedive. This is very common of those who retire too young and don't keep themselves engaged with activity. Our mind's contentment is heavily dependent on the regularity of flow-inducing tasks.

Someone with a more autotelic personality, for example, would be the kind of individual who is motivated specifically by an activity or task, getting more enjoyment out of the doing part than what they'll come away with. They'll carry out tasks, as Csikszentmihalyi says, 'for the sheer sake of doing it'.

This, of course, goes against our cultural conditioning that constantly encourages us to focus only on the goal. This is why people continue to work in jobs they hate because they are motivated only by the end result, the promise of leisure and the perception of status and success. They are allowing the ego to determine what will make them happy 'some day' but what makes the ego happy does not necessarily make the mind happy here and now. People who lead with their ego tend not to place any importance on autotelic activities when as far as your mind is concerned, it's the task itself that holds a valuable piece of the contentment puzzle.

With this mindset shift, you will then need to seek out autotelic activities that, for you, tick the following boxes. You'll want tasks that:

o are neither too challenging nor too easy
o engage your skill set and require that you concentrate but, in the same breath, won't overwhelm you or make you feel out of your depth
o let you feel in control while also letting go of your ego or any self-consciousness
o offer some sort of short-term goal that will give immediate, unambiguous evidence of the progress you're making
o you will derive some kind of enjoyment from.

For those happy in their jobs, it's typically at work where they experience flow. That's certainly the case for me, but if work isn't doing it for you, you can still, of course, achieve it via other, non-professional pursuits.

Unfortunately, though you might want to stop right here and get your flow on, you can't really force it upon yourself. If your mind is distracted and other worries and thought patterns are continually getting in the way, you need to accept that flow is just not happening right now and maybe this particular activity doesn't do it for you. Maybe it does, sometimes, but you've got valid concerns on your mind right now that you need to give your attention to before your brain can enjoy the gentle stretch of flow. Maybe you just need a nap.

If there's nothing that's causing major concern, and you've enough gas in your tank, you'll be able to find the activities that work for you by thinking back over times you've satisfied all of the aforementioned flow criteria. Or, simply take note of times and precisely what you've been doing when you've felt 'in the zone'. And that's flow.

3. Gratefulness

The third and perhaps most powerful psychological tool for contentment is gratefulness (or gratitude). Being completely frank, this is something I used to roll my eyes at. I looked at the idea of a gratitude diary, for example – where you'd make a note of everything in your day that you could be grateful for, from a long hot shower in the morning to a cup of tea when you've come in out of the cold – as a silly exercise that could hardly have any real impact on my very physical experience of anxiety (and the contentment it sucked right out of me). I wanted a quick fix and I wanted it yesterday.

However, as with everything else that now resides in my toolkit, I could no longer consider myself above gratitude once I discovered that scientific research correlates it with increased contentment. For a nice introduction to the simplicity of gratefulness, I turn to David Steindl-Rast (author, monk and lecturer with a voice so soothing it might become an ingredient for contentment in its own right) who said in his now famous TED Talk, that if you really want to be happy, you need only be grateful.

This brilliant man challenges our assumption that happy people are grateful, suggesting instead that grateful people are happy. In this talk, Steindl-Rast says that we all know people who have everything it takes to be happy but they are unhappy – because they want more, or something else. And we know people who have experienced misfortune but are deeply happy. 'Why? Because they are grateful. So, it is not happiness that makes us grateful. It's gratefulness that makes us happy. If you think it's happiness that makes you grateful, think again. It's gratefulness that makes you happy.'

How is this so? When you look at the research (of which there is far too much to squeeze into this chapter), you start to reimagine gratitude as a superfood for life, in that it serves to bolster the three circles essential for well-being: the psychological, the social and the biological.

If we take a look first at the social element, gratitude has been shown, in a 2008 study published on the National Center for Biotechnology Information website, to greatly improve our social connections – and we know social connection is essential for contentment. It helps us to become more empathetic, more of a team player and, generally, you will find that, with increased gratitude, you become a better communicator. Psychologically, our mood benefits hugely from gratitude. We feel more satisfied in the long term.

As explained by Steindl-Rast, when we're grateful, we act out of a sense of enough (what we have), and not from a sense of scarcity (what we have not). In a study conducted by Dr Robert A. Emmons of the University of California and Dr Michael E. McCullough of the University of Miami, researchers asked all participants to write a few sentences each week. One group was asked to make a note of things they were grateful for that had occurred during the same week, while a second group was asked to track their daily irritations or things that had displeased them. The third (control) group was asked to write about events that had affected them with no real emphasis on them being positive or negative. After ten weeks, those who had been bringing their awareness to that for which they were grateful were reportedly more optimistic and felt better about their lives than the other two groups.

From a biological perspective, gratitude actually changes our brain. In 2008, scientist Roland Zahn and his team of researchers carried out the first MRI scan with the purpose of studying gratitude. When participants were asked to summon feelings of gratefulness and appreciation the reward centre in their brains lit up, enhancing the production of serotonin and dopamine, two crucial neurotransmitters that make us feel good. The hypothalamus was also engaged, enabling better regulation of stress hormones. Beyond the brain, gratitude is believed to boost our immune system, release toxic emotions, reduce pain and even help us sleep better, among other things.

For Steindl-Rast, the key to long-term contentment would be to go through our days with constant grateful awareness. We would appreciate each new day, each new moment that presents itself to us, the time we've been gifted and all of the good things we have in our lives. We would even look to challenges and adversities as opportunities. As a result, a wonderful feeling of contentment – he goes so far as to call it happiness – would rise in our hearts.

As nice an idea as that may be, he acknowledges that, unfortunately, life gets in the way. We get pissed off, we get stressed out, we lose sight of what's important, we focus on what we don't have. And that's fine. That's being human. Our negativity bias is a well-meaning but largely unhelpful quirk of our survival instinct. It's how we're wired.

And, so, I would never pressure myself to walk through each day with an overwhelming appreciation for the ground under my feet and the clothes on my back. I don't think I'd get a whole lot done and, let's be honest, if we're too busy noticing the gorgeous blue sky at all times, we really increase our chances of being hit by a bus.

But it is important to give yourself a chance to take your foot off the accelerator once in a while and think about what you're really grateful for, for all of the reasons mentioned above. You can accept your negativity bias because you're never going to get rid of it completely – and you shouldn't want to, because not only does it keep you alive, it consciously chooses to sit with gratitude at least some of the time.

To engage my gratitude muscle, which can get a little rusty when we spend too much of our time in go! go! go! mode, I turn to mindfulness. Apart from the fact that both mindfulness and flow help us to be in the moment, there is a significant difference between the two, and room for both is key.

Flow, which we've just discussed, is the good kind of autopilot, where our analytical and self-talk brain is offline. We need that sometimes; our prefrontal cortex needs a break and our monkey brain needs to be stimulated in a way that isn't threatening but is soothing.

Mindfulness, on the other hand, is what happens when we consciously turn our prefrontal cortex on, switching us out of autopilot mode. We need this too. We become aware of our surroundings, we focus on our breath, we notice how we're feeling in a non-judgemental way and then we bring our attention towards gratefulness.

For increased contentment, Steindl-Rast couldn't make it more simple. The trick, he says, is to just 'stop, look and go', something we were first taught as children when learning to cross the road. Pausing to consider what you're grateful for is a super simple exercise you could aim to do every day or even just once a week to begin with, and it's something that need only last a couple of minutes. I find gratitude-themed guided meditations particularly helpful. I also look for opportunities during the day where I might normally consider myself 'bored', such as queuing for something, and instead use that time to think about what I have, as opposed to what I have not, knowing that it will not only improve my state in that moment, but increase my long-term contentment too.

Of course, there are other psychological ingredients that deserve an honourable mention in this chapter. Self-compassion is a biggie, a non-negotiable contentment essential that we've already explored in detail in Chapter 3. Jump back if you need a reminder. Sure, we can be empowered by our vulnerability, we can foster great social connections, seek out plentiful opportunities for brain-feeding flow and carve out time for mindfulness, but if our daily self-talk is in the gutter, none of this other stuff will matter; we won't raise or embolden our contentment baseline.

PAUSE FOR THOUGHT

With awareness then of vulnerability, social connection and flow, not to mention the importance of self-compassion and gratitude, and how each of these tools plays its unique part in fortifying our contentment baseline, we're slowly shifting away from the stereotypical definitions of happiness, such as more money, a better job, the enviable car or the impressive resumé.

We're looking at what actually makes your brain feel good, instead of what makes your ego feel good, and we're making a point of pursuing that instead.

You might say at this point, with what we now know, that we're halfway to hacking happiness but not all the way, because it's you, ultimately, who has to get you there (and, yes, I know I said I was done with that word but 'hacking happiness' really satisfies my love for alliteration).

Truth #9
Trust your instincts – you have them for a reason

Do you deny your limitations? We all do to some degree. Do you like to think of yourself as not having any? How's that working out for you?

These days, I'm far more accepting and respectful of my limitations than I once was. For example, I fully accept that I will never be the kind of person who can get by on six hours' sleep. I'm not alone in this; less than 1 per cent of the population can sleep routinely for six hours a night without suffering some kind of impairment, according to Matthew Walker, author of *Why We Sleep*. To be honest, I find that even the recommended eight hours is still a bit on the conservative side for me. I feel and perform at my best with a good nine to eleven – OK, fine, twelve – hours of shut-eye. Sure, an expert might say I'm oversleeping, and Robin Sharma might say I could have a whole day's work done before the sun comes up, but I know what feels right for me. Needing my sleep is a limit I have to be aware of but respecting it and working with it is not at all limiting; it's the opposite. It enables me to achieve all that I put my mind to at my own pace and in my own way (as well as allowing for afternoon naps without the guilt).

Similarly, as an anxious person with an extra-vigilant mind, I have found over recent years that it pays dividends to work with the mind I've got, rather than to work against it and try to become somebody I'm not. I tried this for a long time before realising I was getting nowhere fast.

In the middle of writing this book, I had the opportunity to lend my brain to science (while it was still inside my skull, of course) and have my mind mapped by behavioural neuroscientist Dr Michael Keane. With a series of electrodes, some gloopy lube stuff and a frightfully unfashionable hat that looked like something out of a Frankenstein movie, he was able to get a clear picture of how my brain functions. I then had to go on stage, still with questionable slimy hair, and discuss the findings.

Unlike a polygraph test, which is notoriously unreliable, this more sophisticated EEG looks beyond your current state, as you would likely show more anxiety in that moment because you have a scientist looking inside your head. It's not exactly a relaxing experiment. Instead, it studies your brain's longer-held traits or, in other words, the kind of brain you have all of the time and not just in this moment. With just five minutes of data, Keane could see, plain and simple, that my mind is incredibly busy. There is a whole lot of activity happening inside my head, and it's not just now and again, it's all of the time. But it's not exactly fun busy. For a visual, think less wild college party and more army of overbearing parents, out combing the streets, looking for their kids who should have been home by now.

The fact that my brain is busy and vigilant wasn't a surprise to me, nor would it be to anyone who knows me. What was interesting to learn though was that, according to the data, there was some slower wave activity happening near the front of my brain. This is where you'd find the prefrontal cortex - remember the CEO of your brain? - whose job it is to take the information coming at us (all information goes first through the thalamus, as part of the limbic system, and then on to the prefrontal cortex) and decide whether it's something to worry about or not.

Keane, with his neuroscience sorcery, was able to ascertain that my prefrontal cortex has always had to work a good bit harder than the average prefrontal cortex in order to reassure my threat system that everything is OK. In simple terms, I have a mind that is constantly on the lookout for threats and from a purely biological perspective, I'm not so great at calming things down.

A few years ago, this information would have sent me into a spiral. I'd have taken it as a sentencing, that my brain isn't working as a 'normal' brain should and that I would always be affected by anxiety, but now that I have learned to accept my anxious nature finding this out was actually reassuring. It helped me to reframe my limitations in a more positive light, in the same way I've reconsidered my vulnerability as a strength rather than a weakness.

Instead of berating myself for being an anxious person or trying to force myself to be a super-chilled-out person who doesn't get worked up over things (which, let's face it, would require a lobotomy), it showed me exactly what I'm working with, and what I've been dealing with probably all of my life. And so with this knowledge, instead of throwing myself from the frying pan into the fire in the hope that I'd bulldoze through my anxiety, which would have the opposite effect and cause me to suffer, I can accept the limits of my biology (my less than favourable prefrontal cortex) and make it work for me, thus enabling long-term success.

I can do what I can to strengthen my prefrontal cortex to help it do its best, and I can take extra measures to soothe and down-regulate my hard-working stress system (with flow and mindfulness and time spent doing nice, relaxing things) rather than denying it and telling it to just get over itself.

The truth, though it be rather unsexy, is that we do have limits.

On the surface, being told that you have limits can sound deflating and very un-Oprah-like (well, you know I gave up on my hopes of being more like Oprah back in Chapter 1) but here's the thing: it's not about limiting your potential. And it's not that there are things you'll never be able to achieve. Not at all. Rather, it's about limiting the damage you do by pushing yourself too hard and too often into a mould that you don't fit.

Where other schools of thought will suggest you pierce through your limitations in order to achieve the success you're after, forcing positivity and a can-do attitude down your throat when really all you want to do is take a nap, I would like to argue the contrary: becoming aware of and then respecting your limits is necessary to succeed. It certainly is for me, if we're equating success with well-being.

If there's one fool-proof secret to self-care, I believe it is this: we need to stop working against ourselves and start working with ourselves. We cannot evaporate the limitations we face, but we can understand them, accept them and work with them to suit the person we really are. By doing this we become more empowered. What might have seemed like a weakness can be turned into a strength. It's precisely this reframing of my experience that has brought me to where I am now, at a place of ease, well-being and contentment. And I cannot stress how important this is.

I invite you now to think for a moment about your own limita-tions. What boundaries – physical or emotional – do you need to respect? Again, don't see them as weaknesses but rather as helpful clues along your path towards well-being.

Now, you don't have to go and have your mind mapped by a neuroscientist (though it's a lot of fun and I recommend it). If you give it some thought, you're already aware of what these limitations are. They might be physical and thus more obvious. An example would be a friend of mine who had a blood condition that meant his blood would not coagulate if he fell or was hit. Instead it would leak, causing all sorts of problems and he'd have to go to hospital for a transfusion as a matter of urgency. Playing a contact sport wouldn't have been something he could do and though he denied it for a long time, this became a limitation he had to respect for very obvious reasons. When he did, there were far fewer hospital visits and more good times all around. So that's a physical or biological example but our limitations can also be psychological or emotional and, as such, they might be a little harder to identify.

For example, an introverted person will find that too many social activities in a short space of time will drain them of energy, so this is a limitation they would be wise to heed in order to protect their energy. Often, though, they try so hard not to be introverted, because society tells us it's better to be extroverted (however, one is not better than the other). They force themselves into situations again and again that challenge the very nature of their being, which of course creates stress and depletes their energy reserves. They think they should be one way, when, really, they are another way and working *with* this is really what's best for them.

I'm not sure it's an introvert or extrovert thing with me (in fact, I think I fall into the ambivert category, which is a bit of both), but I do know that having too many social outings in a short space of time makes me feel more anxious. Rather than telling myself this is stupid and that I need to push through it or that I *should* be able to cope with it because that's what the world expects of me, I acknowledge that maybe I'm just the kind of person who charges their batteries with nights in and time alone. I respect this about myself and, with that, I balance my time carefully to manage my anxiety. As a result, I feel healthier and more content.

Some limitations are more permanent (like the need for sleep or a chronic blood condition), but others are more transient: for example, you might be well able to take on a side project and do it to the best of your ability in isolation, but when considered in the context of the seven other projects you currently have on the go, you might need to say no.

Similarly, for an introvert, a party might be something you enjoy and feel good about once a week, but less so if it's the third of its kind in as many days and you're not getting that chance to recharge.

Another transient limitation, and one that we've all experienced, would be those times when you've simply run out of gas or, as wonderfully articulated by Sarah Knight in her book *The Life-Changing Magic of Not Giving A F**k*, you've run out of 'fucks to give'; you've exhausted your 'fuck budget'. If you keep taking from this finite resource and pushing beyond these limits, and you don't balance the scales, there is going to be a deficit somewhere, and as we said back in Chapter 3, it's likely your well-being that will suffer.

So far, I've spoken about the importance of respecting our limitations and knowing when to surrender to them. But when it comes to these more transient limitations, I want to make something very clear. It's not always a case of perceiving our limitations as one big red STOP sign that prevents us from ever moving forward; sometimes it is totally fine to proceed, as long as you're aware of the potential limitations and where you'll need to restore equilibrium later on. It's OK to push through limitations from time to time, if it's a push that will serve you well.

With that, you're probably wondering, how the hell are you supposed to know what to do? When should you surrender and when should you push through? When do you stop and when do you go? The answer is simple but one we tend to neglect in our modern world: we turn to the space in between stop and go. We activate what I call our internal amber light.

What's our amber light? I thought you'd never ask.

Essentially, it's how I visualise our intuition. As Viktor E. Frankl famously said, 'Between stimulus and response, there is a space. In that space is our power to choose our response. In that response lies our growth and our freedom.'

For me, in that sweet spot of space between a stimulus and a response, such as being asked to do a favour for someone and automatically saying yes or taking a job that might not be right for you, you'll find your amber light. And by engaging our amber light, not only do we experience the growth and freedom that

Frankl spoke of, we also protect ourselves from doing things that won't serve us well in the short or long term. To understand this amber-light theory, I want you to visualise the colours you'd find on a set of traffic lights. There's only two we're really looking out for when we're on the road: green for go and red for stop. The amber light is what should come between the two, telling us to slow down and prepare to stop with plenty of time but for too many of us, we're simply not paying attention. We're operating with a two-light system only.

If I asked you which light you're most responsive to, and you're anything like me, you'd probably tell me that it's the green traffic light which has the most influence on your life. You're a go! go! go! kinda person. I know I lived this way for a long time. Get this done, get that done. Do it all and do it at speed. Do it before you're ready. Do it because it looks good. Do it even if you don't really want to, because it'll be good for you in the long-run (or so you think). And then this happens: without us even realising, our traffic-light signal switches abruptly from green to red and we have to stop. We have no choice but to stop. What we miss is the amber light that reminds us, gently, when a pause is necessary; it's how we know to start putting the brakes on.

Without this awareness, we find ourselves bumping into what's in front of us. We come grinding to a halt or, worse, we career off the side of a cliff. On the road, the amber light is incredibly important - imagine just how many more road-traffic collisions there would be without it. Well, I like to think that we all have an amber light within us - it's warm glow representing our intuition – and if we gave it as much awareness with ourselves as we do on the road, we wouldn't have half of the stress and anxiety in our lives that we're currently experiencing, we'd be a lot more at ease, doing things that better serve us, at a more doable pace. And we'd be feeling more content too.

But for lots of people, their amber light is either too dim or it's not switched on at all; we ignore it or we don't even have time to consider it. This was the case for me; it seems we only get familiar with our amber light after one too many red-light collisions. From those with whom I've spoken, it seems unfortunate that we have to come crashing through a proverbial red light before we learn to pay attention to the warning signal that would have told us what was coming, if only we had our eyes open. If only we had paid attention.

We shouldn't have to break a light in order to realise how important it is to pay attention to our amber light. It shouldn't be something we retrofit. In fact, it's not something that can work in reverse. Rather, it's a precautionary tool that we can activate right now, that will keep us in check and moving forward. We need to ensure it's switched on and that it's flashing when it needs to. We need to ensure that we can see it, that it's not obstructed from our view – for example, your desire for more money in a job you don't like might block out the requirements of your mental health – and then learn to heed its warning.

But as I said of our limits earlier, a warning doesn't necessarily mean that we have to stop. Don't forget that a flashing amber light on the road is a signal that you can proceed with caution. Sometimes, when your own amber light flashes, it's merely a sign to slow down and look around you. To be aware that it might be safe to go but there are risks associated with your action and you would be wise to take them into account. There may be things to consider – such as our limitations – and weigh up before moving forward.

In essence, by listening to our intuition, which I visualise as a guiding amber light, we're trusting ourselves to do what's best for us. By engaging this inner tool, and really listening to it, we also remove a lot of our daily self-doubt and self-critique because we're giving ourselves that all-important space between stimulus and response wherein true clarity can present itself.

But how do we know what's worth surrendering to and what's worth proceeding with?

Unfortunately, I don't have the answer to this. I can only answer that, for myself, with each junction that I come to, as and when I come to it. What you do will depend entirely on you – your personality, your limits, your current circumstances and your past experiences – and the only way to really know which route to take is to become better acquainted with your own amber light. That I can help you with. It's a tool that we all have; you just need to bring it into focus and then regularly tap into it.

When you learn how to hear your intuition and start to trust it, activating your amber light becomes a lot easier to do on a regular basis.

At first, though, it can be a little tough. Maybe you're too used to saying yes or too used to saying no without pausing for consideration. So, your intuition doesn't get a word in. Maybe you're too used to pushing away what your intuition is telling you because you're concerned with what you *should* be doing. You're too focused on logic and, as a result, you give no importance to that 'knowing' feeling. The most important thing is to practise stepping back and giving yourself a little time to sit with the possibility of something before fully committing to it.

Consider how the possibility makes you feel and let your mind wander where it may. Take a shower, go for a walk, make yourself a cup of tea, scribble into a journal – do anything like this in a quiet space, and your intuition will have a far greater chance of being heard. Listen to the thoughts that come up. Ruminate on them for as long as it takes, sleeping on it if needs be. Allow for the good thoughts and bad thoughts with no judgement – this is mindfulness.

If it helps, you could ask yourself the following kinds of questions: What emotions are you feeling? Intuition and emotions go hand in hand. Does it excite you? Does it scare you but in a good way? Does it make you feel stressed? Does the thought alone drain you? In order for your intuition to answer these questions, and not your ego, your inner critic or your voice of reason, you need to be really honest with yourself about how you feel. Emphasis on the word *feel*. Again, no judgement. Sometimes, you'll answer these questions and you still won't be sure whether to step back or proceed. If you get here, it helps to simply ask yourself, 'Does this feel right?' If something feels wrong for you, whatever you do, don't ignore that feeling.

Activating your amber light checklist:

o Step back, be quiet, don't try to apply logic.
o What is your gut reaction? There is no wrong answer.
o Ruminate on your answer.
o Go for a walk and disengage from digital distractions.
o Return to your journal. What emotions are you feeling?
o Does it feel right? Does it make you feel stressed?
o What do you think your amber light is trying to tell you?
o Is it reminding you of something you've been overlooking, such as how much you've been expecting of yourself?

I've often wondered whether our intuition can ever be wrong. For me, it's pretty damn reliable but that's because I've worked hard to ensure it's firing on all cylinders. For example, your intuition may be partially skewed if you've been scarred in the past by a broken heart. It may tell you to keep away from a potential new love interest when, actually, it would be better to proceed. Again, it's important to really listen calmly, quietly and mindfully to enable your truest intuition to come forth.

If you doubt your intuition, allow yourself to draw on logic. Use intuition (or the signal of your amber light) first and logical analysis second. I like to bring both into the picture in order to limit my chances of being led astray by either one. Both have their place. To bring your rational mind on the scene, you can ask yourself questions such as:

o Is it something you want to do now for your future self?
o In doing it for your future self will you harm your current self?
o And if it suits your current self will it harm your future self?
o Are you doing it for you or for someone else?
o Are there any red flags?
o Are there more reasons to do it than not to do it?
o Will opting in or out matter in five years' time?
o Is it too much for you right now?
o This might be something good on paper but is it really good for you and your personality?
o Is it pushing you too far past your own limits?

I also find it helps to consider things in a wider context.

So let's say you're toing and froing on a new job opportunity. If your intuition, for whatever reason, is telling you to walk away and you're still unsure, then stack it up against your logic. If you then conclude that stepping away is the right decision for you, it's really important that you stop yourself from considering this as a failure and instead try to see it as a success, albeit a silent one. By opting out of something that's not for you, you've saved yourself from the turmoil it would more than likely have caused you. You're doing what's right for you. What's more, while your intuition might be saying no right now, this no might not be forever. It might merely be because you haven't been respecting your limits and now is just not the time. It might also help you to re-evaluate where you're at and where you want to be.

A friend once told me that if I was ever in doubt, I should remember these words: 'Trust your instincts, you have them for a reason.' I didn't really give much weight to this sentiment until I had one particularly bad experience. I was offered a new job and I chose to ignore the amber light of concern that told me this was a bad idea on many levels and I went straight for green, focusing only on logic. Rather than hear out my very valid concerns, I told myself that this is how it's meant to be; we're supposed to be stressed out to the point of being overwhelmed because that's what happens when you're out there achieving things and working hard. That's how you get to success (and, boy, was I wrong). I took the job and to say it didn't work out would be an understatement – it was the catalyst for what I now describe as my mental breakdown. I broke right through that red light with reckless abandon and the aftermath wasn't pretty.

 PAUSE FOR THOUGHT

For so long, I blamed myself for not paying any attention to my amber light. But here's the thing: when it's already happened and you've found yourself on the wrong side of the red light, this kind of thinking gets you nowhere. You have to accept where you are now, as that's all there

is, and then take what you've learned and move forward. For me, it took going against my intuition to learn how important it really is and how rarely, for me, it's wrong.

We have to accept the inevitability of mistakes in life; we will, from time to time, be led astray by what we think we should do, but that's OK. If you find yourself in this position, know that by being here, you will sharpen your intuition and the next time it's called into action, you'll know to listen carefully, balancing your amber light with logic. When you have a bad experience after which you tell yourself, 'You know what, I just knew this wasn't right', you'll find that you're never without your amber light again. You'll consider things very carefully in order to protect yourself, whether it's to do with a job, a relationship or anything at all that impacts your well-being, and you'll trust that knowing feeling. But remember, you don't have to break a red light to know this. You can turn yours on right now.

These days, my amber light is my most trusted advisor, perhaps even more so than logic. It knows me well, it knows my limits and it knows what I'm capable of even when my inner critic argues otherwise. It knows when I should slow down, when I should stop or say no and, having been burned before, it asks me gently that if I'm going to proceed, I should do so mindfully and with caution. It enables me to live a more mindful life, separating what I think I should do or how I should be from that which is really, truly right for me.

Truth #10
There is no end goal

LIKE COMMUTERS passing through Tokyo's Shinjuku Station or New York's Grand Central, most of us spend our lives trudging, one foot in front of the other, towards an elusive 'end goal'. A lot of the time we're doing so unknowingly; we're on autopilot. Somewhere in the back of our minds, we believe that when we reach this magical end goal in the far-off distant future, the stars will finally align and our happiness will reach its apex. Our purpose will be fulfilled. The boxes will be ticked. And all of this stuff we're experiencing right now, the highs and lows, will all make sense.

And so we spend our years thinking it will be totally worth it. We think that if we didn't have this drive towards this end goal, we wouldn't be motivated to get out of bed in the morning. A lot of us endure chronic stress, working in jobs that from day to day make us miserable, or staying in the wrong relationships that have the same effect but we believe are necessary to get us towards that end goal. The end goal may be more money, not having to work as hard, getting married, feeling respected for what we've achieved, some kind of gratification. The picture-perfect life we see on movie screens (well, the ones with happy endings obviously). The life we think looks good. If you're wondering what your 'end goal' is, it's probably been the driving force of your life, certainly your educational and professional endeavours. To figure it out, all you have to do is start a sentence with 'Some day ...' and let your mind automatically fill in the rest.

With hard work, lots of people do get there and that's a cause for celebration. Less fortunate is that almost as soon as they're there – particularly for professional goals – the goalposts shift. 'What now?' they ask themselves.

In retirement, people retreat from their fast-lane, goal-driven lifestyles and assume their 'some day' picture of life. Though they're happy not to be in a job that drains them of time and energy any more, they learn that total idleness, as we've already discussed, turns out to be a terrible idea. It's not the answer. They realise the end goal, as prescribed by capitalism and Western society, and the means to achieve it, really wasn't all it was cracked up to be. They're either on to the next goal, trying to figure out what that is and how they might fill the void, or they wish they could go back in time. Back to when they had lots of time stretching out in front of them. Instead of thinking 'some day', they'd shift their focus to 'this day' and make the most of it.

I decided to finish the book with this particular truth because of all that we've explored so far, it's this that has had the most profound and positive impact on my life. The fact that I've copped on to this idea at a relatively young age – in my early thirties – is one of my proudest achievements, although not one you'd find on paper or at the top of my LinkedIn profile. I certainly won't be winning any awards for it or framing any medals for my wall.

That said, it's a quiet learning that I really believe will stand to me right up until the day I shake off this mortal coil and so I want to share it with you, dear reader.

To embrace it for yourselves, it's going to require the stretching of mental muscles that are perhaps used to going another way. Much like the other neural pathways we've been attempting to carve out in previous chapters, it will feel a little stiff and you'll likely be met with some resistance at first. You'll find yourself trying to unlearn everything you've been taught in life about goals, and going against how most people have been conditioned to live their lives since the start of the twentieth century – in the pursuit of something, someday.

But if you decide to go for one last perspective shift – of course, you don't have to – let me tell you that when you do get there, as was the case for me, you can look forward to Lizzo levels of liberation. Things don't just get easier but infinitely more enjoyable when you live in accordance with this truth. The pressure lifts, and that can only be a good thing. Because pressure, as a friend recently told me, is only for tyres.

The truth goes like this – there is no end goal.

Well, there doesn't need to be and, if I may be so bold as to state it, this could just be the secret to a life well lived.

Here's how it works.

We've seen all of the movies that tell the story of an old man or woman who realises much too late what was really important in life: some variation on the recipe for happiness we unpacked in Chapter 8. But you don't have to grow older or endure something life-altering to enable this shift in thinking. You can just know, right now, that it is logically a smarter and more fulfilling way to live.

To be clear, when you do away with the concept of an end goal, you're not replacing it with an air of aimlessness. Rather, you make a conscious decision to live your life determined by the kind of life you want to have today – not tomorrow, not someday, but today. The way you want to spend your twenty-four hours and your seven days a week. You live life according to your values, what's important to you now and not according to what you think you should be aiming for or how you think you'd like to be introduced at a party. And that, of course, will still require work, effort and the achieving of that which is necessary to fulfil this aim.

I'll give you an example. I met a man a few months ago when I was a passenger in his taxi. We got to talking about work and he told me that he used to be the CEO of a big fancy-pants corporate company. He was very successful, in the traditional sense, and moved among the perceived upper echelons of Irish society.

'Wow', I said, 'that's impressive.' I wasn't all that engaged, if I'm being honest, I was just making conversation, but he kept talking and soon my ears pricked up. He told me that at the height of his career, the economic crash happened and everything fell apart. Unsure of what to do but needing to keep making money, he took to taxi-driving to tide him over until the dust settled and he could get back into his suit and dress shoes. But then, he told me, after a year or so, he realised something. He was no longer stuck at the office until all hours. He was meeting people from all different walks of life and having enriching conversations. He got a kick out of it. He'd made some great friends in the taxi ranks with whom he'd share a coffee each morning. He didn't have any stress to bring home; nothing to keep him up at night anyway. He wasn't under pressure (in this case it really was reserved for his tyres). He was earning enough money to pay his way and then some. Anything beyond that would have been nice but it wasn't essential.

He enjoyed getting up and going to work each day, invigorated by the chance of what that day might bring. He was able to take time to spend with his family and go away on the odd city break and cook a nice meal for his wife (they had almost never eaten dinner together in his previous job). Cooking afforded him opportunities for psychological flow, which is something he had forgotten. He realised that in what he previously thought was the best position to be, he wasn't content, let alone happy. His stress levels had been so high for so long that he hadn't even been aware that being stressed out had become his new normal. He had grown comfortable in his discomfort and he wondered if the end goal he had been driven by all these years was something he even wanted in the first place.

But the taxi-driving was only meant to be a stop gap. Then, when the economy started to pick up, the opportunity for business came knocking again. This time, he was hesitant. Having been so ambitious before, how could he not go back to it? After much back and forth on what was really right for him – and tuning into his amber light – he had a long conversation with his wife. He told her he was sorry, but he didn't want to go back into the corporate world in the pursuit of something some day. As it turned out, he really liked what he had today.

Admitting that he was more content now than before made him feel vulnerable. Was he just taking the easy option? Should he be working much harder? He thought his wife would react badly, mirroring the shame with which he was grappling. She asked him what was really important to him. He listed off everything that his new-found career afforded him: time, satisfaction, social connection and more. He realised this was really the goal and he was already living it every day. She told him he had nothing to be sorry for (while I, of course, cooed in the back seat at the thought of this adorable, mutually supportive couple). And that if they were to really talk about what looks good and what is enviable, what could be more enviable than realising how good you've got it?

He should be thankful for having realised that on his former trajectory there would have been no end goal. He had been fitting a mould that society had expected of him.

And so, finding empowerment in his vulnerability, he continued driving his taxi. He considered it a gift, a secret almost. His new-found contentment became his greatest success. He did choose a different path, but he did so because it worked for him; it enabled him to satisfy what was important to him in life. Not that it mattered what I thought, but to me this man was incredibly impressive and I think about him often. He will now be immortalised in this book and I can't even remember his name. If you're reading this, mystery taxi man, thank you for the life lesson on what's really important, and for the reminder never to judge another person's version of success.

In sharing this man's story, I don't mean for it to sound like a corporate CEO gig is where your soul goes to die and offend all nine-to-fivers. Not at all. It didn't suit him, but it might suit you. It might give you all of the satisfaction in the world. You might feel content and excited whether you're solving a complex problem or seeing your team or yourself progress. If your amber light tells you it's right for you, that's all that matters.

One of my best friends is an actuary. She works an insane number of hours and it's a seriously high-stakes role with millions-of-euro deals hanging in the balance of her performance. It sounds like my worst nightmare. But as tough as it is, she loves it and cannot imagine herself in any other career; it lines up perfectly with her values. These are the kinds of days she wants to have. So, she's not just living for some day, she's living for this day.

I also don't mean for it to sound like we should sack off goals entirely. This is not the case. Within my actuary friend's role, she has set herself some short-term and long-term goals to keep her focused and on track. But if she was hating every minute of it, and the end goal was to make partner, for example, chances are she'd continue to hate it when she got there, in which case she'd have to ask herself, 'What's the point?' More money? Yes, that's always going to be a motivator, but it's not going to make you any more content than you already are, especially when that hedonistic adaptation kicks in. How would this goal measure up with the way she wants to spend her time? It wouldn't.

Goals are important, motivating and exciting, and they help us to figure out our purpose. They're really powerful – as long as the goal you're pursuing is lining up with what's important to you, which is often determined by your core values and how you want to live your life. If a goal you have means that your well-being will suffer, it's not a goal worth having, in my book.

From choosing college courses to taking our first steps in our career, we put ourselves under a huge amount of pressure to have a clear end goal in our mind's eye and, too often, we create this picture based on what we think looks good. Then we forge ahead in pursuit of that end goal without ever stopping along the way to take stock and check in on whether it's still something we want or whether it's worth it.

Often people find a shift in their goals when they come up against adversity, but as with everything else I've discussed, when we equip ourselves with awareness, we don't have to wait for the shit to hit the fan to create the life that best serves us. We're smart enough to do that right now.

A few years ago, however, I did not have this awareness and I needed it to smack me in the face. I was crazy ambitious and very competitive. I wanted to win and be the best at everything and I was far too concerned with perception. I valued perception more than how I really felt each day. I wanted to rise up and up and up the proverbial ladder, regardless of the cost. Eventually, in the pursuit of this end goal that would never be enough, and would always be changing, I tripped over myself. By now, you know the story of what happened next. I had no choice but to quit my job because the anxiety had taken such a debilitating hold over me.

It took a long time to put the pieces back together again but, when I did, I promised myself that whatever I did going forward, whatever turns I would take or avenues I would pursue, my desire to maintain my well-being would always be front and centre. Don't get me wrong, I'm still a very motivated person. I still want to achieve great things. But I am constantly stacking my goals against my values to ensure that I don't lose myself again. More than anything else, I'm motivated by well-being.

'What does the end goal look like for you?' This is a question I've been asked a lot in recent years. I struggle to answer it for a few reasons. I want to say, 'Well, to be honest, I suppose the goal is to keep doing what I'm doing now.' Just to maintain the contentment baseline I've been fortifying these past few years that, of course, my professional pursuits have played a significant role in. This kind of answer often gets a funny response. It's unusual for someone my age not to be thinking of an end goal; we're so used to wanting more. More, more, more. It's also unusual for someone to say that they're actually quite content where they are. Again, we're conditioned to think, *I'll be happy when ...* or *I'll be happy if ...*; it's widely accepted that we're not supposed to be happy yet; it's something that comes, you guessed it, *some day*.

Now, this doesn't mean I don't say to myself, 'I would like for this book to do well' or 'This other thing would be a great achievement to tick off the bucket list'. For one thing, I would like to do a TED Talk because it would challenge me (I would also require a nappy in order to do it, mind you) and I imagine, if it goes well, that the instant gratification and kudos is akin to a gentle back massage, which I'd be lying if I said wasn't also a motivator. Isolated accomplishments and the inevitable knock-backs can come along, and they can excite and motivate me, but I'm acutely aware that my contentment baseline and my self-worth doesn't depend on them.

Any goals I have today are, for the most part, informed by what's really important to me: I want to feel healthy, mentally and physically. I want to sleep well. I want to maintain the relationships that mean a lot to me, where I can make a difference in their lives too. I want to split a pot of tea with a girlfriend as we dissect the latest gossip once in a while. I want to have dinner with my family and resort to a childlike state of little-sister annoyance and I don't ever want to get to the point where we're not lovingly killing each other at the dinner table. I want to not hate getting out of bed in the morning. I want to spend many more days having conversations with my husband and always prioritising dinnertime together. I want to walk my dog dressed like the pigeon lady from *Home Alone 2* and not give a shit about what people are thinking because I know they're not thinking about me. I want to watch Netflix and pretend I'm just resting my eyes when really I'm drifting off into a deep slumber on the sofa because that's how at ease I feel. I want to write books or give talks or produce podcasts that make a difference to someone who can relate. I want to keep learning new things. I want to have French toast midweek. I want to earn enough money to keep doing all of the above and have something of a rainy day fund should I ever need it.

Though that's a long list, they're all fairly conservative goals that don't require being a millionaire or being world renowned and – minus the rainy day fund – I'm already living it. I have no more loftier goal than this, though I wouldn't say no to an ASOS discount code.

The end goal, if anything, is to sustain it. If any goals come to mind that seem promising, yet take from any of the above, I have to question whether they're worth pursuing. If they compromise my well-being, it's a hard no.

In order to avoid the end-goal trap, I suggest you begin by taking an inventory of your current goal list as well as dissecting any end goal you might have.

o What are your current goals?
o If there is an end goal in mind, what is it?
o On paper, play devil's advocate with yourself and challenge the goal – why does it motivate you?
o What do you expect when you get there?
o Are you enjoying the pursuit of that goal?
o Will you achieve it and be satisfied?
o For how long will that satisfaction last?
o Is it worth everything you're doing now?
o Are you really doing this for you or for someone else or for how you will be perceived?

Then take a look at your core values. Strip away the perception or what looks good or enviable and allow yourself to be vulnerable. Nobody is judging you here, this is an exercise you can do alone. And don't feel shamed into choosing values that aren't yours just because they sound more commendable, such as 'giving back to charity'. If having lots of money or being really well known, for example, is high on your priority list, that's perfectly fine. It's one of your values and your goals can be informed by that.

o What is really important to you in life?
o What do you think will be important to you when you're old and grey?

o Should that be important to you now then?

o If you were to die, what impact would you want to have had on the people you cared about?

A little morbid, I know but, trust me, it helps you get some clarity on your values. Your core values should reflect your priorities. They should encourage you to fulfil your purpose. They should help define who you are and want to be.

Then, think about your lifestyle.

o How are you spending your days now?

o How do you want to spend your days?

o How much room is there for the activities that you know will fill your tank?

Now, I know it's not as simple as saying, 'Well, Caroline, I want to spend less time cleaning up after my kids and running a household on top of a full-time job that I hate but can't quit because I need to pay my mortgage.' For a lot of people this is necessary. We've gotta do what we've gotta do and be realistic doing it. But we do have the power to consider how our goals measure up with what we really want for ourselves. We can ask ourselves if the juice of our end goal is really worth the squeeze. And for the goals we do set, we can tweak them to ensure they're satisfying our core values and that, at the very least, they bring us some level of enjoyment.

How does your current lifestyle serve your values? How does your end goal – or any goal – serve your desired lifestyle that, in turn, serves your values? Does making it to the top of the food chain give you the lifestyle that you want? If not, then is it a smart goal for you? If we pursue goals that aren't tailored to us personally, then we're hamsters on a wheel, chasing a finish line we'll never reach - or getting there and feeling short-changed. Let your values, along with the lifestyle you want, be the driving force in your life, rather than an end goal. Not some day, but now.

When your goals, values and lifestyle land on the same page, you can expect the liberation I mentioned at the start of this book.

 PAUSE FOR THOUGHT

Figuring out where you are, the path you're on and where you're headed might take some time, especially considering how much of our lives we spend on autopilot.

Thinking of the values that really matter to you and the lifestyle you know would bring harmony into your world requires a willingness to be vulnerable, as does readjusting your goals to reflect those values. It's not easy to go against what we've been conditioned to think and choose, for example to prioritise a healthier mind over a healthier bank balance, but it's worth doing.

If you're struggling to identify goals that are really important to you, it's safe to assume that creating a mind that is at ease is a goal we probably all share, though perhaps have forgotten, and that would be a worthy place to start.

As for how to go about achieving this particular goal? I invite you to ponder the following words, spoken to me by my friend Tom not so long ago. They perfectly sum up everything I've tried to articulate in this chapter in two succinct sentences. 'You don't think your way to better living. You live your way to better thinking.'

Conclusion

And that, dear reader, is it. Ten simple truths that might just help you get the most out of life. Ten observations about human behaviour, none of which claim to uncover secrets heretofore unknown to man, but which nevertheless remind you that you are always in the driving seat of your own experience. Ten conclusions I have arrived at - not without difficulty - that have hugely turned down the volume on stress and anxiety in my life, while turning up the dial on the good stuff. Ten ideas that come together to demonstrate the power of vulnerability - the very thing we fear most - and the joy of allowing ourselves to be as we are. Ten truths that, if you're willing to embrace them, will allow for a much calmer you.

Granted, you might not be ready or willing to go streaking around your neighbourhood, such is your enthusiasm for stripping back and becoming naked and vulnerable upon reading this book (although there is photographic evidence of me doing exactly this at my own hen party - it was too late when I discovered the security cameras), but my hope is that by now, at the very least, you'll have changed your perspective on the beautiful vulnerability that's common to us all. I hope that like me, you feel an invisible weight lift off your shoulders as you decide to steer your life - and how you move through it - in a more authentic direction. Authenticity not just with yourself but with those around you too. I hope that you feel empowered to question and confront the negative and destructive behaviours and thought patterns that we can all fall into, the ones that don't serve us all that well. But more than that, I hope that you feel equipped with the insights laid out in this book to make the adjustments necessary to create the life you want and the life that's there for the taking.

Some final advice? Keep this book close – it's certainly pretty enough for bedside shelf status, don't you think? – and whenever you feel a doubt creep in, or the fear of vulnerability emerging, dip back into the truth most relevant to whatever it is you're experiencing. Let the words and the sentiment wrap themselves around you. Go crazy with dog-ears and highlighters and let the book get dirty with all the flipping back and forth. Make your own notes in the margin! There's no greater compliment to an author than a battered-looking book. But in your attempt to embrace these truths – perhaps just one or perhaps all ten of them – please approach them without judgement. Not of me (that's fine), but of yourself. In a recent podcast interview I did for my series, 'Owning It: The Anxiety Podcast', I sat down with behavioural neuroscientist Dr Michael Keane. I was already a fan of self-compassion but his words really sealed the deal for me. He said that if self-compassion was a pill, there's not one human who wouldn't take it every single morning, such is its power and positive impact on our individual experiences. And he's a neuroscientist, not a hippie (well, he could be a hippie neuroscientist), so if he has witnessed the positive, visible impact of self-compassion on the brain at a biological level, I'd probably take his word for it.

Be as kind to yourself as you would be to others and enjoy the process of personal development, all the while mindful that we'll never have it all figured out (shout out to truth number 1). We don't need to. Nor are we hoping to reach some elusive end point where everything falls perfectly into place (truth number 10). All we can aim for is a better understanding of why we think, feel and behave in the ways we do, so that we can proactively enhance our experience not just today but everyday henceforth.

(Delighted to sign off on a word as fancy as 'henceforth'. Hopefully my former English teacher, Ms Prizeman, will be reading this.)

Acknowledgements

Thank you, kind reader, for committing to this book and all the way to the acknowledgements too! If you've been with me since book number one, thank you again. Your support, encouragement and feedback means the world to me.

Thank you to my publishers Hachette for giving me yet another opportunity to write what I want to write about. Thanks in particular to my editor Ciara Doorley for her trust and guidance. Thank you Joanna Smyth and Elaine Egan. Thank you to Cathal O'Gara for the beautiful cover.

Thank you to Faith O'Grady, my literary agent for putting up with my 'tell me again, how do royalties work?' questions, and to Amy Buckeridge, my other fairy-godmother-like agent for your ongoing support and advice.

Thank you to Jo Linehan for reading chapters and correcting my course when my own fear of vulnerability creeps back in. Thank you to my family. Thank you to my best friends – you know who you are – for providing me with a willing focus group at every turn, and to Louise O'Neill, an incredible Irish author who always has time to offer advice.

Finally thank you to my husband Barry for letting me be the 'wild card' in the relationship (i.e. the one who gets to flit around writing about her feelings while the other works 9-5). I love you.

Notes

Truth #1: You'll never have it all figured out

Richard Templar, *The Rules of Life* (Pearson, 2015)

Robin Sharma, *The 5AM Club* (Harper Thorsons, 2018)

Truth #2: There's nothing easy about changing your life

Charles Duhigg, *The Power of Habit: Why We Do What We Do, and How To Change* (Random House Books, 2013)

Daniel Kahneman, *Thinking Fast and Slow* (Penguin, 2012)

Kelly McGonigal, *The Willpower Instinct: How Self-Control Works, Why It Matters, and What You Can Do To Get More of It* (Avery, 2011)

Dr Maxwell Maltz, *Psycho-Cybernetics* (Perigee Books, updated/expanded edition, 2015)

James Clear, *Atomic Habits* (Random House, 2018)

Phillippa Lally, Cornelia van Jaarsveld, Henry Potts and Jane Wardle, 'How Are Habits Formed: Modelling Habit Formation in the Real World' (European Journal of Social Psychology, 40[6], Oct 2010)

www.aspireforequality.com

Robin Sharma, *The 5AM Club* (Harper Thorsons, 2018)

Truth #3: You can do anything, but you can't do everything

Herbert J. Freudenberger, 'Staff Burn-Out' (Journal of Social Issues, 30: 159-165, 1974)

World Health Organisation, 'Burn-out an "occupational phenomenon": International Classification of Diseases' (https://www.who.int/mental_health/evidence/burn-out/en, 28 May 2019)

Arianna Huffington, 'Burnout Is Now Officially a Workplace Crisis' (www.thriveglobal.com, 30 May 2019)

Kristin Neff, 'The Space Between Self-Esteem and Self-Compassion' (TEDx Talks, February 2013)

www.self-compassion.org

Matthew Walker, *Why We Sleep: The New Science of Sleep and Dreams* (Penguin, 2018)

Greg McKeown, *Essentialism: The Disciplined Pursuit of Less* (Virgin Books, 2014)

Sophie Leroy, 'Why is it so Hard to do My Work? The Challenge of Attention Residue when Switching Between Work Tasks' (Organizational Behavior and Human Decision Processes 109(2): 168-181, July 2009)

Glenn Wilson/Hewlett Packard Infomania study, 2005

Truth #4: Where there is failure, there is always opportunity

Frederik Joelving, 'How You Learn More from Success Than Failure' (Scientific American, 1 November 2009)

Janet Polivy, C. Peter Herman and Rajbir Deo, 'Getting a Bigger Slice of the Pie. Effects on Eating and Emotion in Restrained and Unrestrained Eaters' (Appetite, Volume 55, Issue 3, December 2010)

Truth #5: A willingness to be vulnerable makes you invulnerable: understanding the vulnerability paradox

Brené Brown, *Rising Strong* (Vermilion, 2015)

Truth #6: Not everyone will like you

Jennifer Guttman, 'Beware: People-Pleasing Behaviors Can Backfire' (Psychology Today, 2 August 2019)

Harriet B. Braiker, *The Disease To Please: Curing the People-Pleasing Syndrome* (McGraw Hill, 2002)

Amy Morin, '10 Signs You're a People-Pleaser' (Psychology Today, 23 August 2017)

Lauren E. Sherman, Ashley A. Payton, Leanna M. Hernandez, Patricia M. Greenfield and Mirella Depretto, 'The Power of the Like in Adolescence: Effects of Peer Influence on Neural and Behavioral Responses to Social Media' (Psychological Science, Volume 27, Issue 7, 31 May 2016)

Dr Pamela Rutledge, quoted by Brianne Hogan, 'What Happens in Your Brain When You Get a Like on Social Media' (SheKnows.com, 4 December 2018)

Dr Sherry Pagoto, 'Are You a People Pleaser?' (Psychology Today, 26 October 2012)

Truth #7: Someone else's success does not take from yours

Dr Robert L. Leahy, *The Jealousy Cure: Learn to Trust, Overcome Possessiveness, and Save Your Relationship* (New Harbinger, 2018)

Dr Carol Dweck, *Mindset: Changing the Way You Think To Fulfil Your Potential* (Robinson, updated edition, 2017)

Dr Tchiki Davis, 'Click Here for Happiness' *(Psychology Today)*

Truth #8: If you want to be happy, you're doing it wrong

Catherine Moore, 'What is Flow in Psychology?' (Positive Psychology, 12 October 2020)

Arne Dietrich, 'Neurocognitive Mechanisms Underlying the Experience of Flow' (Consciousness and Cognition, 13 [4], 1 January 2005)

David Steindl-Rast, quoted by Helen Walters, 'Want to be Happy? Be Grateful: Brother David Steindl-Rast at TEDGlobal 2013' (TEDBlog, 13 June 2013)

Glenn R. Fox, Jonas Kaplan, Hanna Damasio and Antonio Damasio, 'Neural Correlates of Gratitude' (Frontiers in Psychology, 30 September 2015)

Roland Zahn et al., 'The Neural Basis of Human Social Values: Evidence from Functional MRI' (Cerebral Cortex, 22 May 2008)

Truth #9: Trust your instincts – you have them for a reason

Matthew Walker, *Why We Sleep: The New Science of Sleep and Dreams* (Penguin, 2018)

Sarah Knight, *The Life-changing Magic of Not Giving a F**k* (Quercus, 2015)

Viktor E Frankl, *Man's Search for Meaning* (Rider, new edition, 2004)

Read on for an extract from
*The Confidence Kit: Your Bullsh*t-Free
Guide to Owning Your Fear*
by Caroline Foran

This is not a book to read if your aim is to become entirely 'fearless'. I am not, unfortunately, a custodian of a long-kept secret that will forever rid you of all your fears and leave you with the confidence of a lion, strutting his or her stuff with a Kanye-like swagger among the African plains.

Fearlessness is not the goal.

Expecting yourself to never feel fear is as futile as expecting yourself to go through life without experiencing stress. If that's your aim, I wish you luck but I cannot help you. Instead, I will help you to work with fear, and learn to build confidence. We can employ specific strategies that help our fear work for us rather than against us. We cut the bullsh*t.

ANOTHER DISCLAIMER: Opening a book entitled *The Confidence Kit*, you're likely to assume that the person who wrote it is bursting with self-confidence. The kind of person who jumps out of aeroplanes with the same ease that you order your morning Americano. Right? Wrong. But wait. Don't close the cover just yet.

In the interest of transparency, let it be known that the focus of this book is not on the immediate right-here-right-now fear you'd feel if you were standing in front of an axe murderer – that's not a fear you want to get rid of – but, rather, perceived fears, one of which is the fear of failure, that hold us back from pursuing our goals and feeling confident.

EXTRACT FROM *THE CONFIDENCE KIT*

On the subject of transparency, I feel fear – more specifically, the perceived fear of failure – greatly. My self-confidence has been known to pool around my ankles on many an occasion, which might, on a separate note, explain why I've been cursed with cankles all these years.

But let's just ruminate for a moment: let's assume you've picked up this book because you want to become a more confident and courageous person. You're fed up with the fear that holds you back. Well, how could you expect to learn the skills of managing your fear – personal, social or professional – from someone who's never felt the faintest flutter of it? That's like learning how to be a pilot from someone who's read the manual but never actually flown the plane. So, rest assured, I'm right there with you in the cockpit. Being familiar with fear is step one on the road to building your confidence.

In the interest of clarity, it's worth knowing that this is my second book. Maybe my first book, *Owning It: Your Bullsh*t-Free Guide To Living With Anxiety*, enjoys permanent residency on your bedside shelf. Or maybe you've never heard of it – or me, for that matter – but you liked the colours of this book's cover enough to pick it up. (I don't blame you; whoever said we shouldn't judge a book by its cover?) Regardless of *how* you've arrived here, allow me a little room to ramble to ensure that we're all on the same page (yes, pun intended).

My first foray as an author spoke directly to those grappling with anxiety across the full spectrum – from the mild, where you may be prone to bouts of worry, to the extreme, where you temporarily cease to function. The latter was my experience, once upon a time, and it was precisely how I dealt with it that formed the basis of my first book. To mirror a concept (which has been a great source of inspiration for me) put forward by motivational speaker Zig Ziglar in his book *Over The Top*[1], *Owning It* chronicled my path from survival to stability – or, more specifically, from merely existing between panic attacks to feeling well on a daily basis.

This book is the next organic step, informed, again, by my own experiences. Having arrived at a point of stability, the safe ground of my comfort zone, I know that true success, which can come in many forms, lies beyond, on not-so-safe ground and far outside my comfort zone. While I may have a firm grasp on the acute anxiety that controlled me for so long, my confidence as a person out and about in the world, wanting to achieve things, needed work.

Evolving as I do, this book casts its net a little wider and reaches beyond 'anxiety sufferers'. It speaks to those among us who've come face to face with one of the less-than-favourable tenets of the human experience: fear. And, unless you've removed your brain's amygdala, that's just about everybody.

This book is about thriving in spite of your fear because if, like me, you're the proud proprietor of a pulse, you must accept that fear and anxiety are going to come along for the ride. What you'll learn, however, is that fear and confidence are two sides of the same coin – and it's up to you which side wins out.

From surviving to thriving is the most challenging path and one that, for many, is fraught with uncertainty, self-doubt and fear. In keeping with Ziglar's thinking, this is the path that takes us from stability to success.

The final stage in Ziglar's path takes us from success to significance ... This is a jump that I'm still figuring out.

You'll have to let me get back to you on that one.

I should say at the outset that reading *Owning It* is not a prerequisite for reading this book – this is not *Lord of the Rings: The Two Towers* – neither is having anxiety. If you did read my first book and you've mastered the art of managing your anxiety on a day-to-day basis, sitting comfortably at a point of stability, you will find that with *The Confidence Kit*, we're expanding our comfort zones and refining our skills, so that our lives are not defined by the absence of anxiety or any other uncomfortable experience, but by our ability to excel and enjoy success. It's the same way that good health is not simply defined by the *absence* of disease or infirmity, but by the *presence* of vitality and being in a state of complete mental, physical and social well-being; I need to eat well and exercise, nurturing my body and mind so that I can function at an optimum level. I apply the same logic to personal growth.

Whatever your experiences thus far, the only assumption here is that we all meet at a point of relative stability, with a collective yearning to move forward towards success, whatever this is for you – maybe it's giving a speech at a friend's wedding or getting the promotion you've been dreaming of. Together, we are lacking in the self-confidence necessary to pursue our own definition of success, while our fears stand in the way, giving us the middle finger. Dickheads.

Before diving into what this book can do for you, I'd like to give you a brief catch-up on how I arrived at this point.

Back in 2014, where *Owning It* starts, despite having had 'everything going for me', I fell to the floor with anxiety (both figuratively *and* literally). I had a significant breakdown brought on by rather insignificant events spanning several difficult months that would have an enormous impact on my lifestyle, and forever leave its marks – among them, a tendency towards near-constant catastrophic thinking (bad) and a bestselling book (not so bad). My challenge then was to get my head above water; to function as a 'normal' human being and do the more simple things, like leave the house without the crippling fear of a panic attack. I wanted to change my relationship with anxiety so that it no longer defined the parameters of my life. My goal was simple: I had to get back to basics, to reduce the feelings – both physical and emotional – of anxiety that plagued me constantly, to sleep through the whole night, to socialise without the need to flee and, ultimately, to *understand* rather than *fear* my body's stress response.

Having reached the point of stability where I could resume normal daily life with relative ease – one massive roadblock overcome – I was then approached with an opportunity of a lifetime: a book deal. The leap from stability to success beckoned. But when the initial disbelief and excitement – and prosecco – had worn off, I had to contend with a new set of anxieties, including, but not limited to, the following:

o 'Oh sh*t. What have you agreed to? Oh sh*t, sh*t, sh*t, SH*T. Can you really write a book?'
o 'Are you even a good writer?'
o 'Can you write this *particular* book when you still sometimes *feel* anxiety?'
o 'You're not a psychology professional, who are you to tell people how to manage their anxiety?'
o 'Should you not just carry on with your life instead of dredging all of this up?'
o 'Will anxiety define you again?'
o 'Will it be any good?'
o 'Will it be sh*t? Yes, it will probably be sh*t.'
o 'What will people think of you?'
o 'What if your anxiety comes back?'

And so the internal inquisition went on and on and on, demanding my attention most often between the hours of two and four a.m., when my rational, higher-thinking brain was busy resting and my irrational, child-like brain was bouncing off the walls.

Long story short, I wanted to get through it, so I did. I wrote it. It was tough and I was plagued with self-doubt, but I did it. When it was complete, it was a reward like no other. However, being me, my anxieties didn't end there. I realised I had a lot more to learn and a new set of skills to hone, which led nicely to book number two.

Along with the success of *Owning It* came a set of expectations that filled me with a new level of unease. Live national TV and radio, public-speaking appointments in front of hundreds of people, and all the while my anxious brain is shouting, 'But I have anxiety. Did you not read my book? I would rather eat my own arm than do all of this.'

In a relatively short space of time, I went from panic attacks on my sofa and a fear of leaving my house to facing what I, like so many others, had feared more than death itself: public speaking. Was I able for it? Gulp. And that's not to mention the fears and uncertainty around writing the follow-up book that you're reading right now – the process of which confirmed, for me, that second-album-syndrome is a very real thing. (FYI, the irony of having immense fear about writing a book about fear hasn't escaped me.)

But as I dealt with each one of these challenges, I found and developed techniques, tips and practices that helped me enormously. The more interviews and presentations and public-speaking events I did, the more my perceived fears began to shrink. Don't get me wrong, I still, on certain occasions, might want to regurgitate my breakfast at the thought of a broadcast interview or speaking on a podium to a group of people, but now I have perspective, understanding (around why my body behaves in this way) and, most importantly, experience.

In this book, I'll take you through the processes that I use so that I'm no longer afraid to say yes to challenges; something that helps my confidence massively. At the same time, there are occasions when I'm also no longer afraid to say no, which is important too. It's worth noting here that public speaking has certainly been a challenge for me, but for others it can be anything from going to a party to asking someone out on a date. The point is, it's all relative. Hopefully, with this book, you will be able to gain something that will enable you to push beyond the walls of your comfort zone to where success lies.

Up until the release of my first book, I had developed the skills necessary to live with anxiety, but the skills necessary to thrive outside of my comfort zone and my self-confidence in many areas needed work. I had a choice in any given situation: I could submit to the fear and stay comfortable in a cocoon of stability. I could say no to the second book offer, no to the presentations and talks I was being offered. That would be safe and easy. Or, I could brace myself, take control and figure out a practical strategy for owning my fears, all of which would enable me to move closer to success. I could choose to stay behind my mental blocks or I could take them on. I chose the latter, and I'm guessing you will too.

That choice led to a toolkit, which continues to serve me well, and that toolkit is this book. *The Confidence Kit* takes the mental blocks that many of us are dealing with and turns them into building blocks with which you can work towards your version of success (something that depends on your own benchmarks, values and beliefs).

The thing about our fear response is that it's a non-negotiable part of us. For some, it's a major pain in the arse to manage, but by the final page of this book you'll believe it to be part of your success - so it's important to recognise it, own it and address it.

From this point, I have just one request: give up on trying to become fearless. Fearlessness is a false construct. Instead, accept fear as part of confidence. Contrary to popular belief and the physical effects that fear itself can manifest, fear does not negate courage. Nor does it negate confidence. Rather, it beckons it. The question is: Will you be paralysed by it or will you process it?

Will you own it?

A word about what to expect in terms of structure. *The Confidence Kit* is divided into three parts.

The first part explores precisely what fear is - for example, the difference between perceived fear and the fear you experience when you get a fright, why we fear failure and how fear works in our brains. Our fears aren't going anywhere so to really grow our confidence we need to embrace our fear and manage it.

I also look at what confidence is - and courage too - and why perfectionism can be a major roadblock on the road to achieving confidence, among other important topics. I tease apart the concept of the comfort zone and the other states of being that can help or hinder us. I distil the science and psychology surrounding all of this in as bullsh*t-free language as possible, with some expert input thrown in for good measure. Understanding all of this is essential and just as important as the specific confidence-building tools. Why? Because wrapping your head around exactly what you're dealing with – how it works and why it's normal – takes away a lot of the fear factor. For me, I always feel worse when I don't understand where it's coming from. This knowledge, however, puts you in control; it's empowering and a tool in itself.

In Part Two, we get right down to work with the strategies I use as often as is required to help me manage and own my fear. Here, I look at tools, such as 'fear hacking', 'sidestepping' and other tools that are available to us within stoicism and more. I have structured this part so that the tools are listed consecutively. You might decide to follow them in that same order – starting with 'goal-setting' and working through to 'repetition' and dealing with 'night gremlins' – but when you have a sense of things, you might dip in and out of the tools that speak most to you. There are no rules, and you won't always have to apply all of the tools at once. However, I strongly advise wrapping your head around the what and the why of Part One before tackling the toolkit itself.

For the toolkit, be prepared to do the work involved with a pen and paper (go out now and get yourself a trendy notebook) and be willing to take the action necessary to increase your self-confidence in particular areas of your life. The thing is, you can read all the books you want but until you get proactive in the face of fear, nothing will change.

Part Three wraps everything up with some crucial reminders to take forth with you. What if you fail? What should you do? How should you process that? And what if you succeed? Success is the goal but for many of us, we don't know quite what to do with it when we achieve it.

Looking at the contents page, it might seem overwhelming. The good news is, it's totally doable.

Ready to get to work?